the Laws *of*
JUSTICE

How We Can Solve World Conflicts & Bring Peace

RYUHO OKAWA

IRH Press

IRH Press is an imprint of IRH Press USA Inc.
IRH Press
New York

Library of Congress Cataloging-in-Publication Data

ISBN 13: 978-1-942125-05-1
ISBN 10: 1-942125-05-4

Printed in China
First edition

Cover Designer: Whitney Cookman
Interior Image: © jiji / Lover of Romance / KyodoNews

Contents

Publisher's Introduction ... 13

Preface 19

Contemplative Quotes I
What is Justice on the Global Level?

ℐ *Chapter 1* ℛ
GOD *is* NEVER SILENT
The Truth that Transcends Academic Justice

1. One Problem that Lies Within the Education of
   Developed Countries 24

2. Conflicts Between Academic Study and Faith at
   Universities in America

   A movie about a dispute over faith at a university 25
   The main character of the movie tried to prove the existence of God,
   based on the Bible 27

3. Only God Can Say, "This is the Only Way" 28

4. The Voices of God are Now Coming Down

   Happy Science missionary work started from a grain of wheat 29
   Jesus was the one and only person who heard the voice of God
   in his time 30

5. Transcend the Limits of Academics with Truth

   Commonly accepted knowledge is far from God's Truths 31
   The Truth must be strong 33
   God is alive 35

◄ *Chapter 2* ►

CONFLICT *between* RELIGION *and* MATERIALISM

Who Designed the Human Soul?

1. The Repeated Occurrence of Natural Disasters on Earth ... 42

2. Aiming to End Religious Conflicts

The reaction to seeing religious conflicts differs from person to person ... 43

Happy Science is trying to rid this world of various conflicts 44

Modern-day education does not teach about what is invisible 46

Happy Science is now taking on a challenge to launch a global revolution 47

3. Correcting the Mistakes of Theravada Buddhism

Theravada Buddhists believe that the Buddha will never be reborn 48

The Buddha did not deny reincarnation 50

Mahayana Buddhism teaches that the enlightened one will come back to this world to do salvation work 52

4. Who Designed Evolution?

Scientists mistakenly think that the soul is actually DNA 53

All life forms in this world have a purpose 55

5. Religions that Teach about Death Serve the Public Interest

The definition of death is extremely difficult 56

Religious facilities are places to communicate with the Spirit World 57

The simple Truth, which modern-day intellectuals do not understand ... 59

6. Have a Spirit of Devotion to Something Sacred

The world cannot be saved by computers, as realized by Bill Gates 60

We must keep the desire to seek something sacred 62

I want to lead the world to a future that is bright and free 63

Contemplative Quotes Ⅲ
**The Six Worldly Delusions are a
Guideline to Determine Justice at the Personal Level**

◊ *Chapter 3* ◊

PROGRESS *that* STARTS *from* RIGHTEOUSNESS

Politics and Economics Seen from the Perspective of Justice

1. Two Incidents that Occurred in Relation to Islam

Extreme remarks in spiritual messages from Muhammad, recorded just after *Charlie Hebdo* shooting in Paris 72

How should we regard the Japanese hostage crisis by the Islamic State? 72

During his visit to four countries in the Middle East, Prime Minister Abe referred to the Islamic State 73

The spirits of the Japanese key cabinet ministers visited me for advice ... 74

2. Examining the Ways Japan Coped with the Hostage Crisis

Prime Minister Abe's Japanese-style press conference confused the Islamic State 76

"Rescuing human lives" was a message for Japan, while "not giving in to terrorism" was a message for the West 77

The interpretation of the expression, "humanitarian aid," which the Japanese mass media frequently used 78

How did the Islamic State view Prime Minister Abe's visit to the four countries in the Middle East? 79

Both the prime minister and the mass media lacked messages expressing their value judgment 80

3. What is Righteousness in Terms of Politics?

Two ways of thinking that determine justice 82

Muslims believe that there is no Islamic fundamentalism 83

Laws such as prohibition against female education are not Islamic teachings, but its cultural patterns 84

The two Japanese hostages were subject to the principle of self-responsibility 85

What the Japanese hostages should have left as their dying messages 86

In the international community, messages are only effective if they contain a value judgment 87

Putting human lives first is the Japanese creed, as stated by Shichihei
Yamamoto 88

The only way to assess whether something is right or wrong 89

Ever since the American military abandoned its role as the world's
policeman, chaos increased around the globe 90

4. What is Righteousness in Terms of Economics?

Provide people equality of opportunity, rather than equality
of outcome 91

Make the spirit of *noblesse oblige* a kind of culture 93

5. Spread the Thinking of Progress and Prosperity from Japan to the World

Eliminating disparity will not do any good unless you use wisdom 95

Teach how to fish, rather than giving fish.................................... 96

◈ Chapter 4 ◐

The PRINCIPLE of JUSTICE

Ways of Thinking Regarding
"Justice on a Personal Level" and "Justice Between Nations"

1. Justice: The Most Difficult Topic of Our Day

Justice on a personal level is mostly determined by the law 98

Religious themes are at the basis of justice on the issue of
denuclearizing the Middle East 100

Was there justice in the persecution of the Jewish people? 102

Determining justice concerning ongoing problems is a very difficult
thing to do 103

2. Justice Seen from the Standpoint of Religion

Justice on a personal level starts from an awareness as a child of God,
or a child of Buddha 105

Modern political doctrine started from the denial of the Manichaean
dualism of good and evil.. 106

How did modern political reform arise?... 108

Today, "warm-hearted justice" is disappearing............................... 109

3. How to Consider Justice in Debates over the Constitution of Japan

Scholars' misinterpretation of constitutionalism 110

The constitution does not bind the people; the sovereign people
create the constitution 111

Constitutional scholars are confusing constitutionalism with
rule of law 112

The very Constitution of Japan itself is unconstitutional 113

4. The Dangers of Nomocracy and Rule of Law

The opposite of nomocracy is "governance by virtue" 114

Nomocracy can get dangerous if taken too far 115

Creating more laws to restrict freedom will lead to less convenient lives ... 116

We cannot allow the law to live on and the people to die out 117

5. How Justice is Defined in the World

The two major trends opposing each other in the world 119

Mistakes will occur unless people recognize the world that transcends
this world 121

Eliminating economic disparities will kill freedom 122

Is the one-person one-vote parity really fair? 123

"Justice on a personal level" and "justice for the whole" 125

Contemplative Quotes IV
Mass Media's "Right to Silence" Will Mislead a Country

Chapter 5
The GREAT TURNING POINT *in* HUMAN HISTORY

What is Required of Japan to Become a World Leader

1. The Power of Wisdom Required Now

What I feel now, at the 25th Celebration of Lord's Descent 130

With the help of many, I want to bring the Laws to all people of
the world 131

The kind of wisdom you attain is important 132

2. A Spiritual Revolution that Encourages People to Make a Great Shift in Perspective

The two major streams of thought in the world 133

The significance of the Greater East Asia War 134

The term "peace" has different meanings depending on the country 135

3. Understanding the Conflict in Value Systems of the World

Difficult situations the world superpower America will face from
now on 137

German frustration regarding compensation for the financial crisis of
Greece 139

A split has been appearing in the EU due to increased unemployment
caused by fiscal austerity 140

China's actions could lead to the world splitting in the future 141

Neither constitutionalism nor the rule of law is almighty 142

4. The Spirit of a Religious Nation is Required to Become a World Leader

"Democracy without God" and "Democracy with God" 143

Unlike Greece, the Japanese economy is in no danger of bankruptcy ... 144

What the Japanese government must do now is job creation 144

Contemplative Quotes V
Work to Realize Peace Accompanied by Justice

ℐ Chapter 6 ℒ
ESTABLISHING *the* JUSTICE *of* GOD
The Teachings of the Supreme God, Now Needed by the World

1. The World's Value Systems are Now Wavering

American-type global justice is now in question 152

The standard for judgment must be the realization of the greatest
happiness of the greatest number and the happiness of later generations ... 153

Two contradicting ideas in democracy 154

2. Is the Evaluation of Japan in Terms of World War II Just?

Asia's positive remarks on Japan are not reported fairly 155

The reason why I proactively voice my opinions on global issues 157

Even the victor nations cannot change the culture and religions of
the defeated nations 159

The spiritual background of outbreaks of war, and the historical rise
and fall of nations 160

3. How to View Clashes Between Different Religious Civilizations

The significance of the increase in the number of Muslims 162

The reasons for Western men and women joining the Islamic State as
volunteer soldiers 163

Two heroes described in the movie, *American Sniper* 164

The reasons extremists in Muslim countries are driven to acts of
terrorism 166

4. In Order for Japan to Contribute to World Peace

The reasons why the Japanese "Special Attack" Units depicted in the
movie, *The Eternal Zero*, are not considered terrorists 167

I want people to understand the heart of Yamato, which did not
forsake Okinawa 168

Hegemonism that lacks a noble cause is wrong 169

Japan must gain power to protect itself and contribute to world peace ... 171

5. Overcoming Religious and Ethnic Conflicts

Monotheistic religions tend to speak ill of other religions 173

Buddhism and Japanese Shinto recognize various gods; their idea is close to worshiping the Supreme God 174

Judaism seen from the perspective of righteousness 174

The time has come to revise the criteria of justice on a global scale 176

South Korea's slander of Japan contains remnants of its ethnic consciousness 177

6. Realizing Happiness for All Humankind by Establishing the Justice of God

God's justice is revealed in my books, *The Laws of the Sun*, *The Golden Laws* and *The Laws of Eternity* 179

In World War II, the separation of church and state worked negatively ... 181

God's management works beyond the borders of religions in each country 181

The Supreme God desires to realize the happiness of all people 182

Contemplative Quotes VI
Know What is Truly Right

Afterword 189

About the Author 191

What is a Spiritual Message? 192

About Happy Science 194

Contact Information 198

About IRH Press USA Inc. 201

Other Books by Ryuho Okawa 202

PUBLISHER'S INTRODUCTION

For the past twenty years, Ryuho Okawa, Japanese spiritual, religious, political, business and economic visionary and the author of over 2,000 books and over 100 million copies of these books sold worldwide (translated into 28 languages), has published an annual volume of the core of his teachings which has come to be known internationally as the "Laws Series." *The Laws of Justice: How We Can Solve World Conflicts and Bring Peace* is the latest volume of the Laws Series, which is a compilation of six lectures given between 2013 and 2015, reaching beyond the boundaries of academics by making God's revelations a subject of academic study. By considering conflicts in the world, the author depicts an image of how justice should be in the world from the standpoint of God, thereby helping the readers contemplate current affairs and particular topics related to Japan and other regions.

Ryuho Okawa is recognized internationally as a world visionary, thinker, and author with a simple goal: to help people find true happiness and bring justice and prosperity to the world. In 1986, Okawa, after working for a trading company and gaining experience in the United States, founded Happy Science as a spiritual movement dedicated to bringing greater happiness to humankind by uniting religions and cultures to live in harmony by overcoming various barriers among humanity. Happy Science has grown rapidly from its beginnings in Japan to a worldwide organization. Today, it has 12 million members around the globe with centers in New York, Los Angeles, San Francisco, Atlanta, Tampa, Tokyo, London, Sydney, Sao Paulo, and Hong Kong, among many other major cities. This global movement is leading the future of the world—having impact enlightening individuals, religious organizations and governments including a new vibrant political party in Japan. Ryuho Okawa has dedicated his life to the exploration of the Truth. His books cover essential teachings such as how thoughts influence reality, the nature of love, and the path to enlightenment. He continues to address large gatherings throughout the world, having given more than 2,400 lectures and through live broadcasts and TV programs.

Okawa's latest book, *The Laws of Justice* will be published worldwide, starting with English, German, French, Portuguese, Chinese, Russian, Korean, Mongolian and more, amidst a chaotic period in history where there are an unprecedented number of world conflicts. These include, but not limited to, international terrorism; ISIS invasions and their seizing cities and territories in Syria, Iraq, Libya, and other Middle Eastern and Northern African countries; the Syrian Civil War and tragic refugee crisis; the Iranian nuclear deal; Russia's annexation of Crimea and incursion into the Middle East; the military expansion of China and their ongoing economic meltdown; nuclear development and threats by North Korea; and the breakdown in diplomatic relations between Saudi Arabia and Iran as well as between Russia and Turkey. During the eight years of the American Obama Administration, the world order has begun to fluctuate greatly as the American government has abdicated its role as the world's policeman. The volatile nature of the 2016 American election in both parties, a more peaceful American version of the Mid East Arab Spring, may further complicate the international business, economic and diplomatic climate including critical international trade.

By combining six of the author's lectures given in Japan, *The Laws of Justice* has brought together religious, spiritual, political and economic reasoning guided by the Universal Truths to best analyze how world leaders, academic thinkers, and thoughtful readers can reach Okawa's ultimate goal. In Chapter 3, "Progress That Starts From Righteousness: Politics and Economics Seen from the Perspective of Justice," for example, Okawa examines the Japanese government's reaction to the Islamic State's kidnapping and murder of two Japanese citizens and how the spiritual and political definition of justice comes into play here.

The book begins with Chapter 1, "God is Never Silent" and ends with Chapter 6, "Establishing the Justice of God." Perhaps the most noteworthy aspect of the book is that it connects domestic and international government and political events with religious and spiritual values. Contrary to the claim that religions are the source of conflicts in the world, this book argues that religions have the power to bring world peace by protecting human rights and becoming a base for democratic government. Those who oppose this vision should reflect on history including Stalin's Great Purge in the Soviet Union based on materialistic ideology, the great massacre in Cambodia during the leadership of Pol Pot, the purge from Mao Zedong's Great Cultural Revolution, and the exile of the Dalai Lama from Tibet. North Korea abducted Japanese and Korean citizens and today, countless others are being urged or fleeing the country because they cannot endure tyranny. It is quite evident that in countries without religion, human rights are ignored and opposing opinions are restrained.

America, a great democratic country was founded on religious values. The Declaration of Independence states, "We hold these truths to be self-evident, that all men are created equal, that they are endowed by their Creator with certain unalienable Rights, that among these are Life, Liberty and the pursuit of Happiness." Unfortunately, America has faced changes as President Obama revised this in his inaugural address saying, "We are a nation of Christians, and Muslims, Jews and Hindus and non-believers." In this way, democracy is being shaken now, but we should be aiming for true prosperity of democracy from the right religious value because this would be the way to realize the happiness of all people, not the happiness of the greatest number as often claimed in democracy, just as the author states in Chapter 6.

In his lecture on *The Laws of Justice*, Okawa said, "People say there are world conflicts due to religion, but the religion they are referring to is a monotheistic religion. Monotheistic religions are fighting each other." To help resolve conflicts among monotheistic religions and integrate different beliefs, Okawa has launched a religious revolution or a world transformation through activities at his organization, Happy Science. As part of this movement, he has published Spiritual Interview Series, books that contain messages from the spirits or guardian spirits of people who have a great deal of influence in the world. These include a variety of spirits from historical figures such as Moses, Jesus, Muhammad, and Shakyamuni Buddha to recent people such as Franklin Roosevelt, Nelson Mandela, Mother Teresa, and Steve Jobs. These spiritual messages are proof that there are many gods or divine spirits in the Spirit World. In some manner, these books prove that many levels exist in Heaven and that there is diversity among gods or heavenly spirits. The Spiritual Interview Series can also awaken readers to the spiritual truths, which can bring a peaceful end to international conflicts and create solutions for a variety of global crises. To explain this view, Okawa says in Chapter 2 of this book, "When people die, they return to the other world and resume their life as a soul. While the world after death is the Real World, people sometimes come back to this world again." In short, people are born into the world, over and over again, sometimes not in just one particular country but in many countries, and believe in many religions. If you are a Christian now, you could've been a Muslim in a past life. The opposite could be true, too. As such, you can conclude that there's no meaning to religious and ethnic conflicts.

In the lecture he gave in December 2015, Okawa also said, "The reason why I preach 'The Laws of Justice' is to build the world we can believe in. We have the right to live in a world that we can believe in more." It is a common mission between humans in the past, present and future to build the world we can believe in by establishing the Justice of God. This is why we need to fight against atheism and materialism. At the same time, we should be tolerant to and understanding one another in order to create world peace together, no matter what religion we believe in. As for aspects in older religions that are no longer appropriate to the people in this era, we need to learn new teachings that suit us today. *The Laws of Justice* depicts how justice should be in this world from a higher perspective that surpasses differences between religion, race, and culture. By believing in the author's messages in this book, we can accept many gods (divine spirits), recognize that each and every person has dignity as a child of God, and love and forgive one another.

As the publisher of this book, we sincerely pray that the ideas in this book will go beyond political science, economics and other academic fields, and spread far and wide and bring peace to the world.

*Please note that each chapter in this book is based on a lecture spoken in Japanese, in Japan, by the author, Ryuho Okawa. Therefore, some readers may wonder why there are so many Japan-related topics covered in the book. It's true that the author is Japanese and that Happy Science began its activities in Japan, however the content is universal, not ethnic nationalism in any way. Okawa has written over 2,000 books to date, with the Laws series at the core of his teachings. In Christianity, each of these Laws would correspond to the Holy Bible. The Old Testament is a book on history—it contains actual events that occurred in ancient Israel. However, the contents in the Old Testament gave great influence to the ideas, culture and politics around the world. Being a specific example does not mean it lacks a universal concept; rather, in many cases, you could learn universal Truths from specific examples. We sincerely hope that the readers of this book contemplate current affairs and particular topics related to Japan and other regions from such a point of view.

PREFACE

"The Laws of Justice" is a very profound and serious theme; it is the eternal theme of philosophy. In terms of politics, this theme reveals the reason why people forever undergo revolutions in pursuit of democracy. For religion, to seek the Laws of Justice means to continuously seek the true Will of God.

In this book, I give my definition of what is right in respect to current events in international politics, as well as topics in Japanese politics and the comments of the mass media, all which happened around the time I gave my lectures.* The book also includes metaphysical, idealistic and abstract arguments.

As a newborn religion, we have thus fully incorporated international politics into our teachings. In doing so, my position has always been Socratic; I have been revealing things that people nowadays think they know, but in fact do not.

Whether this is a religious book or a work of political philosophy will depend on each reader.

Ryuho Okawa
Founder and CEO of Happy Science Group
December 2015

---

* This book is a compilation of the lectures with additions. See end section.

WHAT IS JUSTICE ON THE GLOBAL LEVEL?

In answering the question, "What is global justice?"
One criterion that can be used to define it
Is whether the people around the world can see it
As global justice.

There are many countries in this world
And each country proclaims its opinions
Based on its own interests.
Then, naturally,
Countries that cannot agree to those opinions
Will give counterarguments or criticisms
Based on their interests.
Sometimes they may be unable
To settle their differences.
However, in most cases,
A country with great power
Would take on the role of the leader
And guide the world.

The strongest nation or hegemony at the time
Would define what justice is
And would apply this throughout the world.
In the modern era,
We have the United Nations,
Which decides what justice is
Based on the opinions or consensus
Of the international majority.

While Japan has been in a position
To take on leadership in the world,
I am sad it has remained unable
To make sound judgments
And promote good values in the world.
If Japan had nothing to say to the world,
Then the Japanese people must feel ashamed.

We must think in the following way.
A nation must first clearly define
What justice is for its own people.
Then, if this definition of justice
Clashes with the ideas of other countries,
The people must take concrete steps
In resolving such differences.
Each country will have the support
Of many other countries,
So in the end, the countries involved
Should all exchange opinions
And decide what justice is on the global level.

From *What is Global Justice?*

Chapter 1

GOD *is* NEVER SILENT

The Truth that Transcends Academic Justice

ONE PROBLEM THAT LIES WITHIN THE EDUCATION OF DEVELOPED COUNTRIES

In 2014 I published *The Laws of Perseverance* (Tokyo: HS Press, 2014) and in 2015, *The Laws of Wisdom* (Tokyo: HS Press, 2015), as part of our Laws series. During these years, Japan and the world, as well as Happy Science, had indeed experienced a period of perseverance. However, those who aspire to do great work always have to endure times of perseverance. If you look at the history of the world, you will see that this holds true in all ages and in all places.

There is one thing that stands out for me during this period. That is the 2014 acceptance speech made by the Nobel Peace Prize recipient Malala Yousafzai, a 17-year-old Muslim girl.

In Islamic countries, extremists destroyed about 400 schools, declaring that it is unforgivable for young girls to go to school by bus without covering their faces, because they should live conservatively and in line with the traditional precepts of Islam. That was the reason why, in her Nobel acceptance speech, she delivered the message, "Why is it that giving guns is so easy, but giving books is so hard? Why is it that making tanks is so easy, but building schools is so hard?"

Thus, some people who belong to certain religions are now working hard to secure their right to receive a more liberal education and the freedom to choose their occupation. This is certainly one path to make things better and a much needed one.

On the other hand, in developed countries, such as Japan and America, a fundamental question is being raised: is this "education" that people have a right to, an ideal one?

It is certainly true that for people in many countries, the "formula to happiness" is to break away from religion, receive an education, acquire skills, take up a profession and be successful in society. This is their ideal way of life. But in countries that are already developed, the reality is that God is being eliminated and religion thrown out of education, under the pretext of making education "academic."

◈ 2 ◈

CONFLICTS BETWEEN ACADEMIC STUDY AND FAITH AT UNIVERSITIES IN AMERICA

A movie about a dispute over faith at a university

Recently, there was an American movie entitled, *God's Not Dead* [released in 2014].[*] It was also shown in theaters in Japan, though it was a minor release. Its title was translated in Japanese as, *Kami wa Shinda noka* [Is God Dead?] and the nuance slightly changed. The Japanese title brought to mind Nietzsche's words, "God is dead."

The movie is about a university student in America who is told to sign a declaration saying, "God is dead" in his philosophy class. Apparently, the story was created based on actual legal cases where people were harassed for their faith at American universities.

In the story, the professor demands all 80 students to write, "God is dead" and sign the statement at the beginning of his class. All the students sign except for one young man who says he cannot because

---

[*] *God's Not Dead* is an independent, Christian-themed movie that resulted in an unexpected success. A sequel, *God's Not Dead 2*, is scheduled to be released in April 2016.

he is a Christian. The professor tells him that he is not asking him to forsake his faith, which should be practiced at church or at home and not brought to his philosophy class at university.

Listing famous names, the professor states that well-known intellectuals are, or were, atheists. He goes on to say that his class starts from the assumption that God is dead and, from this standpoint of agnosticism, he would discuss the ultimate wisdom that these intellectuals have reached. So, he suggests not wasting time debating the existence of a supernatural being.

The professor then strikes a bargain with the student. He says, "If you cannot bring yourself to admit that God is dead for the purposes of this class, then you will need to defend the antithesis that God is not dead. If you fail, you will lose 30 percent of your final grade." And, knowing that the student is hoping to go into Law School, he warns the student to change his mind.

Nonetheless, the student decides to take up the challenge. The girlfriend of the student gets offended and says, "Don't be ridiculous. I'm here at my third-choice school because I have the next 50 years of our life planned out. If you want to get into Law School, you can't afford to flunk this class. Sign the stupid paper and move on." But the student decides to confront the professor squarely, breaking up their relationship.

Under these circumstances, he carries on an intense debate with the professor. In the debate, when the professor talks about how Professor Stephen Hawking explains in his own book, the words "God is dead," the student points out that in the same book on page 5, Hawking says that philosophy is dead. He counters by saying to the professor, "If you're so sure of Professor Hawking's infallibility, and philosophy really is dead, then there's really no need for this class."

This is the storyline of the movie.

Actually, we experienced something similar in 2014. It was when we asked the Japanese government for official approval in establishing Happy Science University. In the movie, the student is asked to hold back his faith in order to complete his course, graduate with a degree, go on to study at Law School and get a good job. We were placed in the same situation as the student; we felt we were being asked to "declare and sign that God is dead."

In fact, the Ministry of Education, Culture, Sports, Science and Technology of Japan did not approve the establishment of Happy Science University, saying, "A university will be approved only if it teaches a curriculum that fits within the current academic standards. However, we cannot approve a curriculum that is based on spiritual messages* that you currently receive from Heaven or high spirits, since that is not academic study." I feel that this was almost exactly the same situation.†

The main character of the movie tried to prove The existence of God, based on the Bible

In the film, *God's Not Dead*, the student fights on his own at the university. His church also gets involved and, in the end, those who have faith come together and declare that God is not dead. In the philosophy class, by the end of the debate, nearly all of the 80 students say that God is not dead. The student wins the debate against the professor and the class loses its objective.

At the beginning of the movie when the student is registering for

---

* See *What is a Spiritual Message?* in the end section.
† Later, in April 2015, a full-scale private educational institution, Happy Science University (HSU) was established.

the class, an administrative office staff member tells the student to consider a different instructor, recommending two other professors. Seeing the student wearing the cross, the staff member says, "You're going into the Roman Colosseum to fight lions. It's your funeral. I don't think you should register for his class." But the student says that it cannot be that bad and decides to take the class. As a result, he is made to prove the existence of God using the Bible.

In reality, some universities do not approve having philosophical or scientific debates based on the Bible. Even America may have reached a plateau at this point. Still, the movie depicts other scenes, including an atheist student from China being influenced and starting to believe in God, as well as a Muslim woman starting to believe in the Christian God.

✑ 3 ✎

ONLY GOD CAN SAY,
"THIS IS THE ONLY WAY"

The previously mentioned Malala said that people need to create a society where women are free from the curse of religion and can get equal education. She also said that she hoped to become the prime minister of Pakistan in the future and that she wished to return home* for the following summer holidays. However, the Taliban extremists declared that they would assassinate her if she came home. This is a terrifying conflict and a truly chaotic situation.

In fact, in the world that we live, nothing exists as a perfect ideal; eve-

---

* Malala fled her Pakistan homeland and sought refuge in the U.K. after being shot in the face by the Taliban extremists in 2012.

rything has complete and incomplete aspects. We live in such a world.

Recently, there was a general election in Japan and one politician used the slogan, "This is the only way"* and went on to great victory. Indeed, this was one political tactic.

However, only God can say, "This is the only way." People who make such remarks are, after all, truly arrogant. What we can do as human beings is to choose a way that we believe is best from a variety of options. If God indicates a different path than one chosen by humans, then the statement, "This is the only way," would be wrong.

ℒ 4 ℘

THE VOICES OF GOD ARE NOW COMING DOWN

Happy Science missionary work
Started from a grain of wheat

In recent years, Happy Science was confronted with two major issues: one concerned education, where we had to prove what academics is and what a university is in the truest sense, while the other concerned politics, where we were tested to see whether religion and faith can open a path in the field of politics. These issues are still far from being resolved.

However, I daresay everything starts from a single grain of wheat. It was the same for me, too. It began with a single grain of wheat. This

---

* In the 47th general election of members of the Japanese House of Representatives in 2014, Liberal Democratic Party leader Shinzo Abe advocated the slogan, "This is the only way to economic recovery."

religion started from a single revelation that I received from Heaven. I attained enlightenment, awakened to the Truth and mastered it. Then I taught about it to other people and those who believed it began spreading my teachings to the people around them. That was how Happy Science became the large religious organization we are today.

A grain of wheat merely left by itself on a table remains a single grain of wheat no matter how many years go by. Even if that grain of wheat were left outside, if just left alone on a rock, it would soon die. Again, if it was left on barren land, it would bear little fruit. However, a grain planted in fertile soil would bear a hundred times, two hundred times or three hundred times more fruit.

This is the true nature of missionary work. Missionary work is the effort of those who believe they carry the seed of Truth, to devote their lives to bear as much fruit as possible in their given circumstances.

There may be times when, unfortunately, the seed lands on a rock or withers under the heat of sunlight. Or, it may fall on hard-surfaced wasteland, where there is no moisture at all. No matter how hard it may try to spread its roots, the roots may wither and the seed may end up bearing no fruit.

Nevertheless, I believe that amongst you, there are definitely some who will be able to spread the seeds of Truth to one hundred, two hundred or even to three hundred people.

Jesus was the one and only person Who heard the voice of God in his time

In the age of prophets in the Old Testament, the prophet himself was the only one who heard the voice of God in his time. The prophet heard the voice of God and conveyed His words to the people and those who believed His words spread the messages—that is how God's teachings have been handed down to the present age.

The same was true in the age of Jesus. Jesus was the one and only person who heard the voice of God. Jesus continued to declare that he heard the revelation and that God spoke through him. He taught people to know the work of the Father by seeing his own work. The disciples could not do exactly the same things as Jesus did. So, God spoke only through Jesus. Then, among those who heard his words, the ones who believed them spread the teachings to the world.

It is said that Jesus was born in what is modern-day Palestine or Israel, a tumultuous region in the Middle East that was home to many matters of confusion. The teachings of someone who had been born in a region amid conflict and war, which still persist after 2,000 years, has spread to Europe, America and even to Japan. The teachings flourished in some areas and not in others. But it is an undeniable truth that those who believed the teachings spread them through their missionary work, increasing the number of believers to one billion and to two billion.

❧ 5 ☙

TRANSCEND THE LIMITS OF ACADEMICS WITH TRUTH

Commonly accepted knowledge is far from God's Truths

I, too, am continuously sowing the seeds of Truth every day. The year 2016 is the 30th year after having officially established Happy Science in 1986 and the 35th year since I attained Great Enlightenment in 1981. Certainly, the one single seed has spread and continues to spread to a large number of people all over Japan and throughout the world.

Nevertheless, as you may feel, it has not spread widely enough. This is because what is accepted as "common knowledge" at the beginning of this 21st century is quite far apart from God's Truths.

When it comes to education, especially in higher education, it is becoming the norm that religious matters such as faith, God and Truth are being expelled, and anything that does not fit under the name of science should not be taught. This kind of thinking may be a great blessing for Muslim girls who are terrified of the Taliban. If those girls could escape a world where they have to cover their faces and feel terrified while studying, they would certainly embrace this thinking as a blessing. However, I believe that removing and dismissing faith from education also results in a loss of something great.

In modern-day politics, too, through the invention of various political techniques and principles, people are now able to make decisions on their own, as if living in a Godless age. That may be wisdom of some sort. Certainly, there have been ages where kings ruled in the name of God. It is also true that, as a result, countless people have suffered under evil kings. Historically, there may have been more evil kings than good ones. To avoid such unhappiness, a system called "democracy" was established.

However, unless we are careful, through the use of human ideas we could move in the direction of destroying the world that God created and even the Truth that God created—the rules of the universe. In the 18th century, known as the age of enlightenment, God and many of His embodiments were "killed," either literally or in philosophy.

This was the result of trends initiated by modern political science.

Humans on earth cannot produce true wisdom to discern good from evil. Rather, it could take hundreds of years or even over a thousand years for them to understand the Truth. For this reason, some may think, "It is better not to speak of the Truth, so that I can avoid being misunderstood by people living in this modern age. It is better to retract the Truth, hide it and just smile to get along well with others." I can understand that an increasing number of people might think that it is a much smarter way of living to hide God's Truth, their faith and religious conviction and to just choose success in their jobs and harmony in this world.

However, this is sad. It is extremely sad.

How did humans come to be? Why are we born? Why do we live? Why do humans have such a long, continuous history? Why do we exist? If academics cannot answer these questions and its only ultimate objective is to live several decades of successful life in this world, then we must definitely go beyond these limits of academics. I believe so.

The Truth must be strong

Truth is not determined by the number of people on this earth, by how many people agree on something, support it and approve it. Truth is already decided in Heaven. The question is whether the people on earth can accept it.

In this world, at times more than a billion people can be held under the sway of a single devil. There are even cases where a group of powerless students stand up to the nation controlled by that devil. As a result, their fight for freedom could be crushed and swept aside because there is no way of winning against the coercive power of organized and systemized violence.

However, the fact that they fought does not go to waste. I believe that their fight becomes a historic act that brings evil to light and leaves many lessons for other countries.

The Truth must be strong. In this world, people with faith and believers of a religion are often considered to be so weak and fragile that they would clutch at a straw. Some may believe such people are unable to think rationally or logically, are incapable of scientific thought, possess low intellect, or are ignorant and illiterate people who need to be guided by people with "proper" academic knowledge. But in this modern age, those who sought God's Truth and have grasped it must become strong.

Happy Science has also been involved in politics for six years now. But our activities have yet to bear fruit. However, I will repeat this to you: there is only one principle.

Will one seed of grain multiply to one hundred, two hundred and three hundred seeds? Will it increase in number? This will determine whether a religion will succeed in its missionary work and how large it will grow to be.

The same applies to other areas. In politics, this would be to increase the number of people conveying God's Truth to one hundred, two hundred and three hundred. This will lead to the manifestation of God's Truth on earth.

This is also true for education. Those who believe in the Truth should not be ostracized. Instead, they should produce true academic achievements by using the Truth, and enlighten others in such a manner. We must strongly push forward these as experiments on our civilization. I believe that showing people this path is the right way.

God is alive

The age of enlightenment has advanced too far that some may believe that they know everything as if they are gods themselves. Frankly speaking, I feel that some of the scholars who are regarded as "geniuses" make proclamations to indicate that they, themselves, have become gods, as another way of saying that God is dead. They believe that they are gods in their own respective fields and therefore proclaim that they have no need for God.

However, there is great arrogance in this way of thinking. The sin of arrogance is that it halts progress. There is still unknown territory that extends far beyond. If they do not acknowledge this and instead think that they have now become the greatest gods in each academic field or political field, they are at a dead end. Humans must be humble. The future opens only when we are in humility.

God isn't dead.
God is alive.
God does keep silence,
But God is alive
And God is loving all the people of the world.
I think so.
Thank you.

THINK OF LOVE AND JUSTICE FROM THE VIEWPOINT OF WISDOM

Love is essential
And to love others is truly wonderful.
To love thy neighbor is quite a difficult task,
But it is very important and,
Historically speaking,
It is an order from God.
We also think, however,
That justice is just as critical.
There are approximately 200 countries in the world,
And a lot of conflicts occur between several countries.
Sometimes these conflicts lead to war.
At such times,
The decision of right or wrong
Should be made from the universal perspective.
That is when we need justice.

The point is,
Love is important,
But wisdom is required to consider
What kind of love you should give to other people.
If there are many evil deeds occurring
Due to influences by evil spirits,
Then such acts must be stopped.
To stop evil deeds is good.
That is justice.

We are seeking wisdom.
We must think of love
From the viewpoint of wisdom.
We need wisdom,
Especially in the relationship between two countries.
It is, however, incredibly challenging.
Every country has its own issues,
And it has its own reasons,
So it's very difficult.

Despite that,
We must seek what is right
And we must establish justice
By dint of wisdom.
We must think about what love is in this context.
"The love for many people"
And "the love on a personal level"
Are slightly different from each other.
No, they are very different.
If a country is destroyed by a lack of wisdom,
Then that is not love.
If an ill-willed country
Intrudes upon other countries
Due to a lack of wisdom
And many people suffer from such an invasion,
Then that is evil.
At such a time,
The United Nations or other great powers
Should stop those evil deeds.
That is justice.

We usually think of love as something personal,
But concerning international politics,
We must seek justice in terms of wisdom
When conflicts arise between countries
Or when there are civil wars.

From *Power to the Future*, Chapter Two: "Love and Justice"

Chapter 2

CONFLICT
between
RELIGION *and*
MATERIALISM

Who Designed the Human Soul?

⚘ *1* ⚘

THE REPEATED OCCURRENCE OF NATURAL DISASTERS ON EARTH

About two years ago [November 10, 2013], I was scheduled to give a lecture in Thailand. But my lecture was canceled because a direct hit from a typhoon the previous month had caused extensive flooding, with an additional super-typhoon forecasted to strike the Philippines and Vietnam. The super-typhoon's final course was quite unusual, considering factors such as the Earth's rotation and seasonal atmospheric conditions. If it followed the usual pattern, it would have headed directly west from the Philippines, come ashore to Vietnam and then on to Thailand, directly hitting the area where my lecture was scheduled to be held. But the typhoon made a 90-degree turn to the right and headed toward China.

Recently there seem to be many floods, and various global areas are increasingly suffering storm damage from rainfall and high winds. It would seem that natural disasters are occurring in parallel to various "fluctuations" occurring in our societies.*

I digress slightly, but there was an earthquake in Tokyo on the morning of the day I gave this lecture.† The building started to shake while I was bathing and for a moment I even considered running out stark naked, but I was afraid that I would cause myself embarrassment, so I decided to wait it out, and it stopped.

Things like typhoons, earthquakes and volcanic eruptions are all

---

*‡ The author conducted spiritual investigations on the reasons behind natural disasters such as typhoons, hurricanes, earthquakes and volcanic eruptions. The result was that such disasters sometimes occur as a form of unpleasantness, warning or punishment for corruptions in society and disbelief, expressed by the divine spirits. Thus, these events are not always natural phenomena.

† This chapter is the transcription of the lecture.

connected‡, so I have the impression that overall something unpleasant is looming.

∽ 2 ∾

AIMING TO END RELIGIOUS CONFLICTS

The reaction to seeing religious conflicts
Differs from person to person

The true opponent Happy Science is fighting against is actually materialism around the world. Materialism is a huge problem, and if we do nothing about it, its proponents will only keep on multiplying. If we look at the current education system and job development, we can see that we are heading for an increase in the number of materialists. Therefore, we must fight against this.

To give a representative example, there is the biologist Richard Dawkins, who became famous as the author of *The Selfish Gene* [1976]. In 2001, all of America was shocked by the 9/11 incident when terrorists from the Islamic Al Qaeda group crashed passenger planes into the World Trade Center, and right after that, Dawkins decided to write a book called *The God Delusion* [2006]. When he saw the terrorist attack he thought, "What a relief it would really be if religion vanished from this world" and, after doing basic research on religion, he furiously wrote about how mistaken religion was, and the book became a bestseller in America.

I used to work in the World Trade Center and, as someone who spent his young adulthood there, 9/11 was a huge tragedy and I felt truly sad. Had the timing been different, I might have ended up buried beneath the rubble as well.

The World Trade Center was originally designed to stand 200 years, so a lease of two centuries was taken out. Many of the tenants also intended to stay there for that long. However, due to the high rent, the company I used to work for happened to move to the midtown area and did not suffer any damage.

While the biologist felt that he had quite enough of religion, when I observed that very same incident, I thought, "This is exactly why a new religion is needed."

The religious conflict in this case was between Christianity and Islam. Because they were founded a long time ago in different places, their ideas and belief systems differ. These differences were passed down unchanged to the present day, an era of cultural exchanges and interactions. This is why these inconsistencies have now become the roots of conflict, causing hatred and conflict between the two.

This made me think, "Now is the time when Heaven's intentions must be made clear and innovations be made in religions. The time has come when a new religion is needed." Thus, the same disastrous event can produce different reactions depending on the individual.

Happy Science is trying to Rid this world of various conflicts

A typical opinion of people who hate religion is that religions are the cause of many wars. In truth, however, wars occur due to this narrow way of thinking that human beings have built up over time and because each religion has been unable to revise its original teachings.

People who follow the original teachings for a long time will not be able to keep up with the changes in society, so they often clash with other people as fundamentalists do. When a new religion is founded, inconsistencies appear between the existing religion and the new one. For this reason, Happy Science is now carrying out various activities to somehow overcome such religious conflicts.

When it comes to religions of the past, to be perfectly honest, after 2,000 years, or 2,500 years, or even more than 3,000 years, we find a lot of their content no longer applicable to the modern-day world. That is why we are trying to revise those points. However, this is not a simple matter; we need a considerable amount of authority to do so. Nevertheless, Happy Science is now taking on this challenge.

Science has developed rapidly in the past two or three centuries. Please note that we do not deny science. We do not consider religion and science to be antagonistic. In old religions, there may be many points that are not compatible with science, but our attitude is this: "If so, we will teach the science of the future. Then, religion and science will no longer be in conflict." In other words, we believe that it is possible to eliminate inconsistencies between religion and science and join forces instead, by teaching how the science of the future should be.

So, we are aiming to fuse together things that clash because of their heterogeneity and to bring innovation to things that have become outdated and are incompatible with modern-day life. We are also thinking about "how things should be now" in order to create a bright future. Happy Science is thus taking action to rid this world of various inconsistencies, confusions and misunderstandings, and to reduce hatred and conflict.

Modern-day education
Does not teach about what is invisible

Nowadays, much education is aimed at fostering scientists, and nearly half the people in the world of education have a background in science. People with a scientific background mainly deal with things of this world, like materials and physical substances. As they spend many years investigating things that can be seen with the naked eye, they sometimes forget about the invisible. That is simply because they have not studied about the invisible world, or because they have not been taught about it.

I admit that doing research in material things has value. For example, an aircraft designer will think long and hard about the kind of fuselage that needs to be made and will consider such things as the materials and the internal construction. It is a matter of course that he does so. It is also perfectly natural for someone who makes cars to be absorbed in physical objects such as the structure of a car body, or how to build a car that is safe and fast, or how to come up with a good design. I do not intend to say that is meaningless.

However, even though it is fine to be immersed in material objects, we must always remember that we have a spiritual aspect and have a soul in the deepest recesses of our mind. After all, we must not forget our essential nature as a soul, and we must not attach ourselves to worldly things alone.

Happy Science approves the idea of making this world more convenient, and we certainly encourage that. We have no problem at all with high-speed bullet trains or jet planes flying through the skies. The world becoming a more convenient place does not bother us in the slightest. Nor does it bother us that there is an abundance of food;

we think it is wonderful that there is a wide range of occupations. We fundamentally agree with such endeavors. However, we also teach that as a result, we must not allow ourselves to lose sight of the spiritual aspects, or of the existence of the soul, which is our true nature.

Happy Science is now taking on a challenge To launch a global revolution

While positively affirming scientific progress, Happy Science is also trying hard to prove that the soul exists by publishing books, including a series of spiritual messages.* It is a very basic thing to do, but never before in the history of humankind has such an extensive collection of messages been revealed from a diverse range of spirits. From an "all or nothing" perspective, these spiritual messages are demanding all humankind to decide whether these are true or false.

Since people in general cannot confirm that spirits exist, they do not express an opinion about this matter, and instead keep silent. However, our every effort is in fact gradually leading people throughout the world to accept the existence of the Spirit World without them realizing it.

If you think that producing spiritual messages can be done through fiction, please go ahead and try. I doubt that you will be able to. The messages from the spirits have all been made public, which is proof of their authenticity. We do not task 200 or so staff members to research and write each of our books. Any writer will surely understand how unrealistic that endeavor would be.

Recently, it has been very common for us to produce one book with spiritual messages that we record in one day. This is a very ar-

---

* See *What is a Spiritual Message?* in the end section.

duous task. Any writer will understand very well how hard it is to form the contents of one whole book with a single interview. We are continuing to produce these spiritual messages to accumulate a large body of proof. This is the challenge of Happy Science, and in a sense, we are trying to launch a global revolution.

ℐ 3 ℛ

CORRECTING THE MISTAKES OF THERAVADA BUDDHISM

Theravada Buddhists believe that The Buddha will never be reborn

Looking at the situation of the world now, the Islamic world is starting to be shaken by waves of liberalization, and the Buddhist world is shaking slightly as well. Even in countries like India, some news outlets report that the number of believers in modern Buddhism is increasing, not just in Happy Science. This shows that people are looking toward Buddhist ideas and teachings to break down India's caste system. So, there is great appeal for Buddhism.

Countries such as Sri Lanka and Thailand still adhere to Theravada Buddhism, but this branch of Buddhism is also in urgent need of considerable structural reform. It is wonderful how the original fundamental teachings of the Buddha have been faithfully passed down in Theravada Buddhism, but misinterpreted parts have also remained and have strongly taken hold.

Simply put, the problem with Theravada Buddhism is this. If carried to the extreme, it states, "This world was created by demons, so being reincarnated on earth is nothing but a suffering. Then the best thing to do is to become enlightened and enter nirvana; then you will no longer need to return to this world." In other words, it teaches, "Since this world is ruled by demons, the highest form of enlightenment is to attain a state in which you do not need to come back to this world. The Buddha entered nirvana, so he would never come back to this world again."

It is incredibly difficult for me to go to places where this kind of faith has been established. I want to go and give a lecture in Thailand, but 95% of the people there firmly believe that the Buddha does not reincarnate, which really makes it hard for me to lecture there.* Moreover, it is also difficult to repudiate this belief entirely. Theravada Buddhism has existed in that form for more than 2,000 years now, so denying it may work to destroy that traditional culture altogether.

Japan and Thailand are promoting amicable relations as Buddhist nations, and we are also developing our connection economically. What is more, around two-thirds of foreign investment in Thailand is from Japan. These cordial relations must be maintained, so we need to think about to what extent we should become involved with their traditional culture. If we say straightforwardly, "The Buddha was reborn. The Theravada Buddhism that you practice is mistaken, so abandon it," it would provoke a genuine uproar. So, we need to carefully consider how to explain the Truth.

In any case, the translations of my books on Buddhist teachings have been delayed in Thailand, so we must lay the groundwork by

---

* The author attained Great Enlightenment in March 1981. In July of the same year, the Buddha consciousness appeared from deep within the author's subconscious and told him that he is the rebirth of Buddha [see *The Laws of the Sun*](New York: IRH Press, 2013). When the author gives his lectures, he spiritually senses the collective thoughts of the audience and speaks on topics that they need. This is why he cannot speak nearly as freely when speaking to the people of Thailand, who do not believe in the rebirth of Buddha.

pushing forward a little harder with translations in languages such as Thai.*

The Buddha did not deny reincarnation

Sri Lanka is also a Theravada Buddhist country. Yet, when I went there to give a lecture, large numbers of monks came to hear me speak, even though we had announced beforehand that those who do not believe in the rebirth of Buddha are advised not to attend the lecture [see Figure 1]. Perhaps this is because Sri Lanka is rather close to India.

Thailand adopts a system where almost all boys become a monk for a few months, so many people experience the practice of Theravada Buddhism. During this time they lead the life of mendicant monks, their heads shaven and their bodies wrapped in orange robes, and they practice ancient teachings that have remained unchanged for 2,500 years, such as "You must not marry," and "You must not touch money with your bare hands." From this perspective, Japan and

Figure 1.
On November 6, 2011, the author visited Sri Lanka and gave a lecture in English entitled, "The Power of New Enlightenment." 13,000 people attended his lecture, of which 90% were Theravada Buddhists who did not believe in the reincarnation of Buddha. But he taught them straightforwardly, "Devils deny the reincarnation of Buddha; He is their enemy." As a result, about 70% of the audience (10,000 people) became members of Happy Science.

---

* Later, in September 2015, the Thai translations of *The Laws of Great Enlightenment* (Tokyo: HS Press, 2014), *The Rebirth of Buddha* (Tokyo: Happy Science, 2009), and *The Essence of Buddha* (London: Sphere, 2002) were published.

other Mahayana Buddhist countries may appear extremely corrupt and tainted.

On this point, I feel I must somehow change their conventional thinking. In all discussions, there are essential elements and non-essential ones, so it is not good to emphasize non-essential points while not stressing the essential ones. Even if they firmly adhere to things like manners and minor precepts, it is pointless if the essential elements are missing.

For example, there is a huge problem if people think that returning to the other world after death and entering nirvana means striving for "nothingness." The Buddha taught the concepts of "breaking free of the cycle of reincarnation and entering nirvana in the Real World." Translating this into words that are easier to understand, he was in fact saying, "Essentially, this world is a transient one, and the other world is the Real World. We are born from the Real World into this transient world, which is the school where we learn. We then return to the Real World after having refined our souls." So, what he was saying is simple: the other world is the Real World.

Therefore, he does not mean that this world should not exist, or that one should never be born into this world again. That is not what is meant, but some people are mistaken on this point. In fact, the concept, "The Spirit World is the Real World" does not mean, "This world is ruled by demons" or "This is a world that we do not want to be born into." But if people strongly believe so, then they are mistaken and need to be corrected in their thinking. I am now pondering how we should teach people this Truth.

Mahayana Buddhism teaches that the enlightened one Will come back to this world to do salvation work

So, why do some people dislike the thought of the Buddha returning to this world so much? This is something I cannot understand. Who would benefit if the Buddha does not return to this world? That is what I would like to ask them.

Who would benefit if the enlightened one would never return to this world again? It would be those who would suffer when the Buddha gives sermons. Then, who are the ones that would suffer?

Given that they believe this world is ruled by devils, never returning to this world again would mean the same as promising not to interfere with the world of devils ever again. It would be like handing over a written oath to leave the world of devils alone once you have attained enlightenment.

However, there is something strange about such enlightenment. It would mean that those who have attained enlightenment would leave this world for good and would never concern themselves with the world of devils. This would be the same as a policeman, for example, promising to stay away from a certain house, no matter how often it is burglarized. There is something wrong with that.

So, we can conclude that there must have been some form of misinterpretation during the process of compiling the Buddhist sutras and the spreading of the teachings. Furthermore, this misinterpretation has fused with materialism that has gained power in modern times. In other words, more and more people regard materialism as being more scientific, and feel that it is unscientific to believe the existence of souls, that believing or having faith is something to be ashamed of. Therefore, materialism has also become alloyed with this idea.

Thus, despite the fact that 95% of the population in Thailand are Theravada Buddhists, we need to somehow alert them and awaken them to the Truth. Those who do not want the Buddha to return to this world are controlled by devils. And they would indeed be in trouble if he returns. However, in order to find salvation, people need the one who gives the teachings to come back to this world periodically.

On the other hand, the True Pure Land school of Buddhism teaches that the enlightened one no longer needs to come back to this world for soul training, but will do so to do salvation work out of compassion for all living beings. This is probably a revision made by Mahayana Buddhism, which I believe is generally correct.

It is true that there is much impurity and suffering in this world. But you should not just try to get rid of your attachment to this world; you should rather try to cleanse this impure world as much as possible. This is an important task. Helping many lotus flowers bloom in muddy waters is valuable work. I sincerely hope people understand that the Buddha did not forsake this world.

ℐ 4 ℒ

WHO DESIGNED EVOLUTION?

Scientists mistakenly think that the soul is actually DNA

From a materialistic or a scientific point of view, it is possible to expose various kinds of "errors" in the religions of the past. For example, Richard Dawkins, whom I mentioned earlier, was accusing Christianity in the books he wrote after 9/11.

He writes that a doctor or biologist should provide proof of the idea that Jesus was born of the Virgin Mary. If he were the son of the Virgin Mary, then a DNA test should prove that he only had genes passed down from a woman, and none from a man. He also poses some questions such as, "You say that Jesus brought the dead to life, but can a doctor or scientist accept this as a scientific fact?" and "Which doctor can verify that Jesus was placed in his tomb and was resurrected three days later, after which he showed his face to other people, walked and ate a meal? Is that possible? And can you really believe that even though he had been resurrected, he flew up into the air and vanished?"

Of course, during the course of time there are many aspects of the story of Jesus that have been broadly interpreted as mythical. But I still think there is a problem in the way that Dawkins criticizes those aspects.

As a counter opinion, I would say as follows. It would indeed be difficult at this point in time to verify whether Jesus had any of his father's DNA. But this man Dawkins says that the soul is actually DNA, which is a succession of chains, or a combination between a man and a woman. This statement makes me want to say, "Hold on!"

People started talking about DNA in the 20th century, but it already existed even before we knew about it. There was no factory inside the mother's womb where the baby was formed with magic hands, nor was there any kind of programming to input a blueprint of the baby. We do not know why, but the baby is formed in the womb. This is a mystery that cannot easily be explained.

Regardless of whether you know about DNA or not, you cannot explain how a mechanism where humans bear babies, who then grow into adults, had long been established. In the evolutionary argument, there are many aspects which people can only seem to explain as happening as the result of a string of coincidences.

All life forms in this world have a purpose

In truth, if you look at the life forms of this world, you will find that there is a purpose for all existence. All life have traces of the purpose for which they were created. Life was created according to some kind of blueprint.

So, who drew up the blueprint? Who made it possible for humans to move and live as such, based on a blueprint? Can it be explained? Certainly, it does not just happen accidentally by the accumulation of dust or the blowing of wind.

There is a view that states, "Masses of protein formed in a primeval ocean, started to move and became human beings" but this is too warped of a theory to believe. It is already known that primeval Earth was searingly hot, molten and burning at an incredibly high temperature. There can be no doubt that it was an extremely hot planet made up of exploding volcanoes and molten lava. So, there is no way that any trace of life could endure in such a place. Or, some people may say that meteorites came flying from space and brought with them tiny bacteria that then evolved. But it is impossible that they developed into human beings as we are now purely by coincidence.

Thus, although it is all right to insist that you only believe things based on proof, and while I admit that there was indeed some form of evolution, the truth of the matter is that all living things have a certain degree of rational purpose. It is impossible to deny the existence of a Being that designed and thought up the story. I therefore believe that there is a problem in completely denying divine will.

✑ 5 ✒

RELIGIONS THAT TEACH ABOUT DEATH SERVE THE PUBLIC INTEREST

The definition of death is extremely difficult

What about the resurrection of the dead, as written in the Bible? It is a question of whether one accepts it or not, and there are actually some doctors even today who accept this. For example, a professor at the University of Tokyo has written a book saying that human beings are souls, and placed advertisements of the book in newspapers. Furthermore, it has been confirmed that human beings sometimes come back to life; sometimes a doctor's determination of death is not accurate. It is extremely difficult to define death. Death is not necessarily something that has to be verified at a hospital, as the determination of death is very difficult even for doctors.

I teach that while the soul and the physical body are still connected by a silver cord, that person is alive and there is still the possibility that he or she may come back to life. This view was also taught in the time of Plato, but it has been forgotten today.

Modern medicine cannot even understand the basic human construct, that a soul and a physical body are connected. Therefore, there is a problem in deciding everything based on modern medicine. It needs to put more effort into clarifying the mechanism between the soul and the physical body. Moreover, psychiatry is stuck at a rather undeveloped level, so it also needs to be studied much further.

Religious facilities are places to Communicate with the Spirit World

Things could appear differently depending on the aspect under focus. So, we must consider this point carefully. As I mentioned earlier, materialism from the scientific perspective is rampant today, and in the same manner, there is also a fairly popular view in the Buddhist stream of thought that states, "Nothing remains when humans die." This view happens to match people's needs, when they are having difficulty building family tombs due to increases in land prices.

More and more people are now scattering the ashes in the mountains or over the sea, believing that there is nothing left after death. It certainly is economical since no grave is required. If they believe there is nothing after death, it certainly makes good economic sense; it is possible to save millions of yen at least. So, from an economical point of view, it is understandable that people would want to believe this.

However, the truth is that a grave functions as a kind of "antenna," while it may take a different form or shape in the West than from the East. In other words, people visit a grave or pray in front of a Buddhist spirit tablet and, by adopting this method of offering prayers, a grave will serve as an intersection through which the mind of the person praying can be attuned to that of the dead who is in Heaven or in Hell. In that regard, the grave is truly important.

Average people are not mediums, so they can rarely communicate with the dead whenever they feel like it. However, if the deceased expect the bereaved family to hold a memorial service for them, such as on the anniversary of their death, and the bereaved family does so out of a wish to offer them a prayer by gathering at a particular place, such as the graveside, then their hearts will be attuned to one another.

Their feelings for each other will be communicated as if they are connected via telephone.

In fact, once souls have returned to the other world after death, they are usually busy with their work there. But from time to time, they recall their descendants and wonder how things are going. At that time, if there is an occasion where they can meet with surviving relatives, such as a memorial service or some other ceremony, they can recall those people fondly. If there are such memorial services, the deceased too can hold on to their memories for several decades, though in most cases, they will gradually forget about this world. This is why it is better for there to be some way to make contact with this world, as long as their family and friends are still alive.

Happy Science shojas, such as Tokyo Shoshinkan, our local temples worldwide, and our religious facilities such as the "Happy Afterlife Memorial Park" are also venues for communicating with the Spirit World [see Figure 2]. These facilities are therefore not meaningless. Interaction with the Spirit World really does occur at these places. In this regard, religion truly serves the public interest but many people are unable to acknowledge this aspect of religion that cannot be seen.

In this world, if you market mobile phones or smartphones, you

Figure 2.
(From left) Happy Science Tokyo Shoshinkan, Happy Afterlife Memorial Park (a cemetery in the grounds of Nasu Shoja, in Tochigi Prefecture, Japan).

will be able to sell millions or billions of them in no time, but unfortunately, it does not work like that with crucial matters that lie at the core of being human beings. Many people are skeptical or do not believe in their importance. This is truly sad.

The simple Truth,
Which modern-day intellectuals do not understand

Compared to people in olden times, people today have become wiser in many ways and are probably also more intelligent. There can be no doubt that their brains work faster, or that they possess more knowledge. However, it is a great shame that they live without knowing the simple and basic Truth.

The Truth is very simple. In short, it is as simple as this: "When people die, they return to the other world and resume their life as a soul. While the world after death is the Real World, people sometimes come back to this world again," or "People undergo soul training in this world on earth, then they shed their physical body and, after their funeral, return to the original world that is the Real World. And those in the Real World are watching the people in this world."

Even people who, in worldly terms, seem to be very clever, or who have attained various achievements or have won prizes, do not understand this simple Truth. Many intellectuals consider it to be an extension of primitive man's animism or of ancient people's nature worship. That is why I am now proving that what they consider to be a "delusion" is not in fact so. This is a battle; the Truth cannot be defeated.

There are many religions in the world, and the people who believe in them far outnumber unbelievers. But religions also contain inconsistencies. While ancient religions contain inconsistencies from a modern perspective, if we were to add appropriate explanations and properly teach people which parts are allowed to be revised, then I am sure they will be able to understand. There are actually many parts that can be changed, but it is also true that there are some common Truths that must be preserved.

✑ 6 ✐

HAVE A SPIRIT OF DEVOTION
TO SOMETHING SACRED

The world cannot be saved by computers,
As realized by Bill Gates

I have spoken about various matters. Fundamentally, Happy Science is trying to create a free and open society. We are trying to ensure freedom today, as well as in the future, but at the same time, we also seek the Truth. There are basic rules of how human beings should live according to the Truth, and we are helping people observe those rules, making sure they do not head in the wrong direction.

In reality, however, there are people who have chosen the wrong direction and are now suffering in Hell. I would like you to know that for those people, no matter how famous, clever or rich they may have been in this world, these aspects are meaningless.

A while ago, I read a special feature on Bill Gates in a certain English newspaper. He had already stepped down from direct management at Microsoft and is now mainly working with his charitable foundation. He charitably spends more than four billion dollars a year on healthcare, food and various kinds of infrastructure in poverty-stricken regions in Asia and Africa. Spending more than four billion dollars means that he wields more influence than the average religion. Thus, he is now using the money he has made to fund his charitable foundation.

Bill Gates expresses his opinion as follows: "There are still too many people who do not realize that just connecting to computers will not save the world. The younger generation of people living in today's computerized world all think that the world will develop and prosper by computer connectivity, but they really need to know that in fact, there are many people who cannot be saved by computer access.

"The people starving to death in Africa cannot be saved. The people dying due to a lack of medical equipment cannot be saved. The people dying of diseases such as polio cannot be saved. And unless dirty water is made clean, the people who catch intestinal disease from unsafe water cannot be saved. Computers cannot save these people." This is what he says.

Although computers seem to be widespread in India, once you get three miles outside the city, you will find yourself in a world where computers are of no use at all; you will enter a world where there is an extreme shortage of goods and many other things. In reference to this, Bill Gates comments something like, "Mark Zuckerberg, the founder of Facebook, says that the world will greatly develop and change if around five billion people are connected to the Internet, but that's just not the case. Zuckerberg says things like that because he hasn't seen society as it really is."

Thus, Bill Gates has now realized that there are people who cannot be saved solely by computers. In this way, he has been developing a religious mindset. Steve Jobs previously criticized him for not having this mindset, but now he is doing this charitable work with sincerity. So, he is trying to use the huge amount of money he amassed to contribute to society. Thus, wealth can be a power to save the world, so I do not deny wealth altogether.

We must keep the desire to seek something sacred

Looking back, Happy Science has made considerable progress in our fight to spread the Truth over the past 30 years or so. However, we still have not spread it to all corners of Japan, and we do not yet have enough power to save the world. Even so, it is true to say that Happy Science activities are now starting to influence the Islamic world, the Vatican and materialist China.

The next age is coming. Ideas that were thought to be real and true, but were in fact nothing more than mirages, are crumbling simultaneously all around the globe, and a new world is about to come into being. That is why we are now making various efforts to change the world. This includes battles in our main work of religion, in the world of politics, in the world of business and economics, battles through educational reform, battles through arts and battles through various other activities around the world. We are certainly exerting an influence, but we still do not have sufficient power.

With the current school education and vocational training, the number of materialists will only increase. This is because people do not have knowledge about spiritual Truths and, even if they do, some people are unable to speak openly about religion or faith, so they tend to keep it a secret.

There is a Japanese cartoon series entitled *Saint Young Men*. The premise is that the Buddha and Jesus are living out normal, everyday lives in Tachikawa, Tokyo. While Japanese readers find such content amusing and it has been fairly well received in Japan, non-Japanese people find it insulting and offensive. From my perspective, too, I find the content to be disrespectful. For example, there is a scene where children shoot rubber bands at whorl of white hair on the Buddha's forehead saying, "That's his weak spot." Little knowledge is better than none, but still, this cartoon goes too far. People need to know just how low this level is.

We need to have a spirit of devotion to something sacred. Invisible things cannot be observed under the microscopes used for research, or seen through a telescope, but if people have lost the holy attitude to imagine what lies beyond what they can see with their eyes, that means they have lost the sacred aspect as human beings. This puts them on the same level as an animal, or even brings them to the level of a machine, which is lower than the level of an animal. We need to keep the desire to seek something sacred in order to resist this trend.

I want to lead the world To a future that is bright and free

The battle against materialism is still continuing. In China, religious activities are still kept under surveillance despite the liberalization of its economy. Even so, the number of underground Christians is now said to have increased to around 100 million. Therefore, we can assume that their political system will break down in the near future.

Amidst all this, I would really like to spread the Happy Science faith there as well. I want to save people, not defeat them. South Korea too still remains in spiritual ignorance, as does North Korea. There are also many autonomous regions that are under Chinese control, but with the emergence of the Internet, it has been revealed that many independence movements are occurring in various locations.

China keeps making accusation about how Japan was a bad country more than 70 years ago, when they have actually invaded and dominated other regions.* From a global perspective, it is not fair that they are condemning Japan while keeping silent of their own deeds.† If they want to say how the Japanese committed evil deeds in the past, they should do so after properly returning the territories they have invaded and recognizing the autonomy of these territories. That would be fair and understandable. However, to conceal their acts and say, "Japan did wrong, but we haven't done so" is an unforgivable act as human beings.

I want to fight against these kinds of current issues. And I will definitely lead the world to a future that is bright and where liberty is guaranteed. I will keep fighting for liberty. What Hitler hated most was liberalism, which means he and I are complete opposites.‡ This has always been my message. Please do not misunderstand this.

---

* The People's Republic of China has historically invaded its non-Han neighbors and ruled them as "autonomous" regions. In 1947, China incorporated a part of Mongolia as Inner Mongolia Autonomous Region, in 1955, East Turkestan as Xinjiang Uyghur Autonomous Region and in 1965, Tibet as Tibet Autonomous Region. Currently, China is conducting policies that ignore human rights in these regions—banning the use of local languages and religious worship and heavily oppressing independence movements—which are attracting international concern. On the other hand, China has been calling out to the international society for the past few years on Japan's so-called Nanking Massacre Incident in 1937 in which its troops are said to have massacred 300,000 Chinese upon capturing Nanking. However, the authenticity of this account is questionable; some say that the population of Nanking at the time was around 200,000. According to the author's spiritual research, this so-called Nanking Massacre did not even exist. See *What Really Happened in Nanking?: A Spiritual Testimony of the Honorable Japanese Commander Iwane Matsui* (Tokyo: HS Press, 2015).

† Happy Science has continuously investigated the significance of the Japanese Army's fighting in World War II through spiritual messages, readings and so on. See books such as *The Truth about WWII: Justice Pal Speaks on the Tokyo Trials* (Tokyo: HS Press, 2015) and *The Truth of the Pacific War: Soulful Messages from Hideki Tojo, Japan's Wartime Leader* (Tokyo: HS Press, 2014).

‡ Happy Science is a religion that prioritizes freedom and tolerance. The author, who is also the founder and CEO of Happy Science Group, has long been criticizing totalitarianism and national socialism. Its political party, the Happiness Realization Party, says that Japan must become a great country of freedom.

THE SIX WORLDLY DELUSIONS ARE A GUIDELINE TO DETERMINE JUSTICE AT THE PERSONAL LEVEL

By checking for the Six Worldly Delusions,
Which consist of greed, anger, foolishness,
Conceit, doubt and wrong view
It can be determined whether a person is
Possessed by evil spirits.
Greed means to have too much desire.
It can be seen in people who make you think,
"This person is really greedy."
Anger means to go into a rage
Or to have a really short temper.
Foolishness means to be unwise.
It is the "ignorance" that Socrates talked about.
It means to have no knowledge of the Truth.
Conceit means to have too much pride.
It means to be full of yourself,
Quickly becoming arrogant.
It is when someone claims himself or herself
To be superior.

Doubt means to be overly skeptical.
Some journalists are suspicious of everything.
Indeed, to a certain extent,
Questioning can be a method
For discovering the Truth,
But basically speaking,
You cannot develop a human relationship
With someone who doubts everything.
People who are overly skeptical have gone too far.
Wrong view means
To have a completely mistaken faith
Or to be caught up
In a mistaken philosophical thinking
Or a mistaken creed.
For example, it means when somebody says,
"Marx is indeed a god"
Without any hesitation or guilt.

Have deep conversations with the other person
And see if he or she has any
Of these Six Worldly Delusions.
If there are two or three
That really stand out in him or her,
Generally, you would be right to consider
That person to be possessed by evil spirits.
Then, tell him or her, for example,
"You are mistaken on these points,
So you might be possessed by evil spirits,"
"Perhaps it would be better for you
To study the Truth,"
And "If you do, your mind will be at ease
And the evil spirits will immediately leave you.
You will become cheerful
And feel the light pouring into you."
This will also serve as life counseling.

In this way,
You can guide the other person
Through life counseling
By checking for the Six Worldly Delusions
In him or her.
The Six Worldly Delusions can be used as a guideline
To determine what justice is at the personal level.

From "The Principle of Justice" Q&A

Chapter 3

PROGRESS *that* STARTS *from* RIGHTEOUSNESS

**Politics and Economics Seen from
The Perspective of Justice**

✑ *1* ✎

TWO INCIDENTS THAT OCCURRED IN RELATION TO ISLAM

Extreme remarks in spiritual messages from Muhammad, Recorded just after Charlie Hebdo *shooting in Paris*

In this chapter entitled, "Progress that Starts from Righteousness," I would like to discuss themes that are rather controversial. There has been a series of incidents related to Islam since the beginning of 2015. On January 7, 2015, there was the *Charlie Hebdo* attack in Paris.* Muhammad expressed his opinions on this incident in a spiritual message.† His remarks were so extreme that our staff at General Headquarters were frozen in shock.

I truly feel the perplexity of the matter. In particular, Japanese residing in Japan are unable to align their thinking with ways that are different from their own because they are stuck in their own unique and limited ways. This is what makes things more difficult.

How should we regard The Japanese hostage crisis by the Islamic State?

About two weeks after the Paris incident, a Japanese hostage crisis by the Islamic State occurred. The Islamic State captured two Japanese men as hostages, with a message uploaded on the Internet demanding

---

* Muslim extremists attacked the office of French satirical newspaper *Charlie Hebdo*, which had published a series of controversial cartoons of Muhammad. Twelve people were killed including two policemen.

† This spiritual message was recorded on January 15, 2015.

that the Japanese government pay a ransom of 200 million dollars within 72 hours otherwise the two would be killed.* This completely overwhelmed the Japanese government. I intend to speak theoretically to help you understand the matter more clearly.

During his visit to four countries in the Middle East, Prime Minister Abe referred to the Islamic State

This hostage crisis appeared to be an extremely unpredictable and puzzling incident. In general, I had the impression that the Japanese mass media treated it similarly to a domestic kidnapping case, where a criminal takes cover and demands a ransom. I felt that there was no difference in the way the government dealt with it.

But this incident occurred when Prime Minister Abe was visiting four countries in the Middle East. It was very timely. The endangerment occurred while he was there, so of course it must have been well planned ahead of time.

In his speech in Egypt, Prime Minister Abe declared that he would donate a sum of around 200 million dollars to the countries contending with the Islamic State. In the speech, he used the expression, "in order to help reduce the threat ISIL poses," which implied that he wanted to drive the Islamic State into a corner.† But after the hostage crisis, he modified his declaration saying that it would be non-military assistance and desperately tried to withdraw any connotation to

---

* The two hostages, Haruna Yukawa and Kenji Goto were eventually killed one by one, but later on February 2, 2015, their spirits came to Happy Science Master's Holy Temple to communicate their feelings through spiritual messages. These messages are included in *A Spiritual Interview with the Leader of ISIL, al-Baghdadi* (Tokyo: HS Press, 2015).

† In his speech, Prime Minister Abe said, "In order to help reduce the threat ISIL [the Islamic State] poses, we will offer our support to Turkey and Lebanon and also provide aid to the refugees and displaced persons of Iraq and Syria. To those nations battling with ISIL, we pledge a total of 200 million USD to aid in the development of human resources and infrastructure."

military connection.

The news about the hostage crisis came out when he was in Israel. Apparently, he received the first report at around 2:50 PM [Japan time] on January 20 and saw the screening images of the hostages at a hotel.

The spirits of the Japanese key cabinet ministers Visited me for advice

That morning on January 20, 2015, Happy Science ran a large advertisement of a book on the spiritual message from Muhammad in the morning edition of the *Asahi Shimbun* newspaper. It was bad timing because that very afternoon, the Islamic State broke the news of the kidnapping. I was afraid that a difficult situation had arisen at a rather complicated time.

I thought the book was not sufficient to explain what was going on, but since my schedule was full, I did not have time to produce another book to explain the situation further. In addition, the hostage crisis was expected to end within three days, so I did not voice any opinions from my standpoint right away.

Thus, although it was unusual, Happy Science did not give any information on the matter. However, just after lunchtime on January 22, the guardian spirits of the key cabinet ministers who were working to settle the matter at the Prime Minister's Official Residence visited me one after another. At that time, the government stated that they would take all possible measures to settle the issue. Seeking my advice that way was, no doubt, one of the "all possible measures."

They did not actually call me on the phone, but their guardian spirits came to ask me, in anguish, as to what they should do.* These spirits included those of Prime Minister Abe and the Chief Cabinet Secretary, as well as the Minister for Foreign Affairs. But the first one to appear was, for some reason, the guardian spirit of the Minister of Education, Culture, Sports, Science and Technology, Mr. Shimomura [at the time of this lecture].

The guardian spirit of Mr. Shimomura looked quite wearied, so I asked why he had become so feeble. He answered, "I'm in trouble now. People are telling me that we are cursed because of me."†

The guardian spirits of the other ministers asked for my opinion on the issue and as to what they should do to solve it. But I just replied to them, "This time, I do not intend to give you an answer."

Actually, we had the right to refuse. For a long time, we had been carrying the risk for everything by telling them what to do and by convincing the media beforehand. Then finally, the government would slowly take action, saying it was their plan from the start. This had been the pattern of their behavior for so long that, this time, I told them, "Once in a while, you should think for yourselves and take responsibility for your decisions. If we tell you what to do, you will make us bear the responsibility, won't you?"

Usually, when I voice my opinion and the government follows my advice, the mass media keeps quiet and does not attack the government. I realized that the government was trying to have me give a lecture on the issue so that they could use the same approach again. So,

---

* When a person thinks about someone else for an extended period of time, his guardian spirit [a part of his subconscious] spiritually influences that targeted person. Here, the author tells how he spiritually detected the guardian spirits of Japanese ministers who came to seek political guidance. They came to him because he has been stating in his lectures and books, as the national teacher of Japan, on how Japanese politics should be.

† In 2014, the Minister of Education, Culture, Sports, Science and Technology disapproved the official establishment of Happy Science University and apparently, he considered this as a cause of a curse.

I thought, "Let's see who can hold out longer" and told them to think for themselves and did my best to resist them. Nevertheless, I found that there were important points that they should know in relation to this issue, so I decided to communicate them.

✑ *2* ✒

EXAMINING THE WAYS JAPAN COPED WITH THE HOSTAGE CRISIS

Prime Minister Abe's Japanese-style press conference Confused the Islamic State

Prime Minister Abe learned about the news of the Japanese hostage crisis while visiting the Middle East and held a press conference in Israel, which was quite unusual. At the press conference, he made two points: first, "We will give top priority to human life"; second, "We will not give in to terrorism." But he did not answer questions regarding exactly what they were going to do. This response was very typical of Japanese, but apparently, neither the prime minister nor the Japanese government was aware of that.

My impression from a third party perspective was that Prime Minister Abe's talk must have dumbfounded the terrorists, including the one wielding the knife in the video claiming responsibility for the kidnapping. When they heard that Japan would give human life top priority, they probably thought the ransom would be paid. But when they heard next that Japan would not give in to terrorism, they must have thought, "So, they're not going to pay? Does that mean they will take military revenge?" When the question was finally asked as to what to do, the prime minister just answered, "We will do everything we can to resolve the issue." Hearing this, the terrorists must have become totally bewildered, because logically, they had no idea as to what exactly Japan would do.

In fact, non-Japanese people would not understand this "Japanese logic." However, the problem was that the person speaking could not see how illogical his comment sounded to others.

"Rescuing human lives" was a message for Japan, While "not giving in to terrorism" Was a message for the West

Prime Minister Abe's first message—"We will give top priority to human life"—was meant for the Japanese people. He had to say it for the Japanese voters through the reports of the mass media, because if he did not, he would lose in the election and his approval rating would go down. That is why he said that he would give human life highest priority. His next message, "We will not give in to terrorism," was directed toward the West. He was telling the Western countries that Japan would not give in to terrorism.

He did not answer the question as to what they would do, which means he actually had no solution against the people holding the hostages. He only said that the government would do its best to resolve the issue, without providing any details. We could only assume that Japan would negotiate to reduce the ransom behind the scenes, but he probably did not have an answer.

The interpretation of the expression,
"Humanitarian aid,"
Which the Japanese mass media frequently used

Through the mass media, the Japanese government tried its best to emphasize that the 200 million dollars was actually humanitarian aid and would not be used for military purposes. They urged the media to report this. It seemed to me that this was to persuade the terrorists not to execute the hostages. However, the terrorists had accurately grasped what Prime Minister Abe said in Egypt, so it was doubtful whether the government would be able to persuade them in that way.

Materials and supplies are absolutely vital in military affairs, so offering financial assistance is virtually the same as fighting alongside one another. In this sense, it seemed to me that the Islamic State understood the information accurately.

The Japanese mass media, including NHK [Japan Broadcasting Corporation] and various other TV stations and newspapers, all reported at the time that it was humanitarian aid, believing that by doing so they could get the hostages home. In my view, however, I thought that their claim would not be enough to convince the terrorists.

That is because the Islamic State was also in a situation where it needed such aid. Around that time, thousands of people had already died from air raids in the Islamic State, including civilians who were not soldiers. They were probably thinking, "If you're talking about humanitarian aid, what about us?"

It is clear that the money Japan distributed as "humanitarian aid" was not given only to countries that took in refugees from Iraq and Syria like Turkey, but also other countries like Egypt and Israel. The Japanese media used the term "humanitarian aid," believing that it would sound like having nothing to do with military action, but I thought it would be surprising if the negotiation went smooth; I actually doubted that the terrorists were convinced. Rather, I thought that even though Japan was trying to say there was no military connection to the aid, the Islamic State would not interpret it that way.

How did the Islamic State view Prime Minister Abe's visit To the four countries in the Middle East?

In fact, what the Islamic State wants the most is money, especially to fund its military. It employs many soldiers who have come from other countries, initially attracting them with high pay. But now that the price of oil has been halved and a lot of the oil wells and many buildings have been destroyed by American air raids, their infrastructure has been heavily damaged. So, of course they want money.

One of the two Japanese hostages was a journalist, Mr. Kenji Goto. His family had actually been receiving threatening emails from the Islamic State, demanding a ransom of one billion yen [approx. eight million dollars], then two billion, since the end of 2014. The Ministry of Foreign Affairs of Japan had received that information, so when Prime Minister Abe went to the Middle East he already knew that two Japanese were being held hostage. While knowing this, he visited the Middle East and distributed money. I assume that this involved negotiations asking for the cooperation of those countries since Japan's hands were tied.

Thus, the incident was not a mere coincidence. Although the Japanese government knew of the hostages in 2014, the prime minister went abroad and gave out money in the Middle East. Generally, this would mean that Japan sided with the countries opposing the Islamic State, thereby becoming its enemy. I am afraid that the Japanese government did not understand this point well.

Both the prime minister and the mass media Lacked messages expressing their value judgment

I have pointed out several problems concerning the Japanese government's response to the hostage crisis. In short, Japan was missing one crucial point: they did not mention one single word about right or wrong. Put another way, Japan did not make any comment showing its own value judgment of the kidnapping. This is a trait very typical of Japanese.

Countries such as the U.S., the U.K., France and Australia have carried out air strikes against the Islamic State because they judged it as evil. Usually, the act of killing someone is wrong by nature and is regarded bad from the perspective of good and evil. But because these countries saw the acts of the Islamic State to be unjust and wrong, they believed the use of air strikes would be justified. These countries are actually making a value judgment here.

The Islamic State, on the other hand, has its own particular logic and reasoning for its action.* Ever since the Iraq War and the Arab Spring,† there has been a reversal of power; those who had been in advantageous positions previously now face very difficult situations

---

* On January 31, 2015, we conducted a spiritual research on the true intention of al-Baghdadi, who calls himself a caliph and the leader of the Islamic State. Refer to Ryuho Okawa, *A Spiritual Interview with the Leader of ISIL, al-Baghdadi: Including a Spiritual Investigation into the Truth of the Japanese Hostage Taking* (Tokyo: HS Press, 2015).

† The Arab Spring was the wave of large-scale demonstrations and protests against governments that began from civil resistance in Tunisia (Jasmine Revolution) in 2010, then spread throughout the Arab world.

and have nowhere else to go. In these circumstances, the Islamic State emerged in an attempt to create a new authority. What is more, the Islamic State is aiming to bring together and unite the Muslim world, so that it can create a vast domain with a power that extends as far as Northern Africa and Southern Europe. Their thinking is typical of the ideas held during eras of war.

Whether the Islamic State will actually be recognized as a "state" is doubtful, but their way of thinking is attracting volunteer soldiers from all over the world. For this reason, the judgment of good or evil on this matter is a very difficult issue.

Japan is trying hard to send the message that it bears no ill will toward Islam. However, this alone is not a sufficient explanation for providing them financial aid, because there are different countries in the Islamic world, some of which are disputing or even combating one another.

NHK reported on several Islamic mosques in Japan and showed scenes of Japanese-speaking Muslims in various locations praying for the release of the two Japanese hostages. NHK might have done this knowing that Muslims in Japan have assimilated the Japanese way of thinking and will say only what are acceptable in Japan. This is an example of the entire Japanese mass media working together to make sure that their reports would not work against the government's effort or stand in its way. Unfortunately, the major problem was that no one gave a value judgment on the overall issue.

✑ 3 ✌

WHAT IS RIGHTEOUSNESS
IN TERMS OF POLITICS?

Two ways of thinking that determine justice

Another point I want to add is the matter of justice. We have to think about justice, or what is right and what is wrong.

With regard to justice, there are roughly two different ways of thinking in the world. One is that justice is in the hands of God. That is to say, people believe that only God can decide whether something is in accordance with justice; the decision is in God's hands, so humans cannot make the determination. This way of thinking is firmly rooted in religious countries.

Another way of thinking is that justice is determined by humans through a democratic process. People put God aside and believe that justice is determined by the law, which was created by representatives elected through a vote, in the legislature or the Diet. Anything that goes against those laws, decided by the majority, is wrong, while anything in accordance with them is in line with justice. There is this kind of thinking.

Then, there is also a stance in between. Some democratic nations decide justice based on their assumption of what the Will of God would be.

So, does the determination of justice only lie in the realm of God or can humans determine justice? This is where the two major value judgments actually collide. Please know this.

Muslims believe that there is no Islamic fundamentalism

There are thus two different approaches, but both have problems. For example, even members of the Islamic State prostrate themselves and offer prayers to Allah just as other Muslims do, so there is no doubt that they are believers of Islam. However, they just act based on what they believe Allah would do, so the truth is they do not understand the Will of Allah. In other words, although they say that God determines justice and they take actions believing that their thinking is in line with God's thinking, in reality they do not actually know the Will of God. They act based on their own assumption, so we can never be sure whether they are truly in accordance with the Will of God.

On the other hand, countries like the U.S. and the U.K. carry out air strikes on the Islamic State. France had also declared that it would send an aircraft carrier after the Paris shooting. Australia has taken part in the air strikes as well. Basically, the Christian countries have concluded that Islamic fundamentalism and radical Islam are evil, separating the extremists from moderate Islam and drawing a line between them. This is their basic way of thinking.

From the perspective of Muslims in general, however, there is no such thing as Islamic fundamentalism. There is essentially no fundamentalism in Islam, so they are perplexed when they hear the words and will ask, "What is Islamic fundamentalism?" If you tell them that it is the modern reenactment of the thoughts and actions in Muhammad's era, then they will say, "What is wrong with that? There's nothing wrong with that, because nothing has changed since then. That is exactly what we are all aiming for." If you ask how they see Islamic extremists, they will simply say that these people are passionate and pure-hearted.

Some Islamic countries engage in business with the West, receive financial aid from Japan and station Western troops in their territory. From the perspective of so-called "Islamic fundamentalists" or "Islamic extremists," these countries defile Islam. They see such countries as overly compromising, being heavily imposed upon and poisoned by Western civilization, or Christian culture. In this way, there is a slight discrepancy on both sides.

Laws such as prohibition against female education Are not Islamic teachings, but its cultural patterns

There is another aspect of Islam that is easily misunderstood from the Western perspective. In France, for example, wearing headscarves is legally banned in public places such as state schools. The Western view on Islam is that the teachings prohibit women from receiving an education and make them wear a headscarf, and that extremists and fundamentalists behave violently to those who go against the teachings.

However, there are no such rules in the Islamic teachings. There are no teachings such as, "Women must wear a headscarf" or "Women must not receive education." Actually, these are set by paternalism or the patriarchal system. Put simply, the father has all the authority within a family, similar to how things used to be in many countries, including Japan. The whole family is ruled under the father's ways of thinking. These standards are the result of a cultural pattern, not religious teachings. Therefore, it is not right to say Islam is wrong just by referring to these behaviors.

The two Japanese hostages
Were subject to the principle of self-responsibility

As shown, there are many aspects that make justice very complex, especially if we are to consider whether incidents align with justice.

At the time of the Japanese hostage crisis, many people tried their best at the crisis management headquarters in Jordan, as well as in Japan, working day and night to resolve the issue. I feel sorry to them for saying this, but speaking bluntly, the two men taken hostage entered the Islamic State at their own risk.

At least, journalist Kenji Goto knew the danger; he filmed a video before he left saying that he would take full responsibility for his own actions and would not resent the Syrian people no matter what might happen. Moreover, he asked not to blame them for anything that might occur. The other man, Haruna Yukawa, went there to do research for a private military company he had established. Both men entered Syria for a work-related purpose, so they must have anticipated the danger of being captured. From this, we must say that the principle of self-responsibility surely applied to them.

If they entered Syria despite knowing the risk involved and with no intention to cause trouble for their mother country Japan, they should have kept their dignity even after being taken hostage. If they had been told to say their last words in Japanese, I wished they had said what should have been said, as Japanese men, based on the samurai spirit.

Overall, the disgracing aspects of the Japanese stood out in this hostage crisis. That is how I felt. I had the impression that the Japanese people could not really clarify where the responsibility laid, the limits of how far people are allowed to go and how much responsibility the government should bear.

What the Japanese hostages should have left
As their dying messages

In the case of American and British hostages, before they are executed, they are told to say, "The American government is to blame" or "The British government is responsible." When the Japanese were taken as hostage, I wished they would cry out for the Japanese Self-Defense Forces to come and rescue them, if they had been told to leave a dying message before being killed.

This would have been the most effective way and a powerful force to change Japan. I truly wanted them to say, "Why can't the Japanese Self-Defense Forces come and rescue us?" This would have been the best thing they could have done. If they had done so, Prime Minister Abe may have paid up 200 million dollars. That is because it is so hard to change the Japanese public opinion.*

According to Western thinking, Japan should have tried hard to find some way to rescue the hostages. Since the Japanese Self-Defense Forces have commando units, they could at least have been flown there. From the Western point of view, the commando units should have landed in Turkey or Jordan, at the very least.

Because of the abductions by North Korea,† for quite some time the Japanese Self-Defense Forces have undergone training where they parachute down on rescue missions. During this hostage crisis, they

---

* The Constitution of Japan heavily restricted the use of arms by the Japanese Self-Defense Forces [JSDF], even in its missions to rescue the Japanese living in foreign countries. This had continued for 70 years since the end of WWII due to strong opinions and politics by peace-loving people who were against war. However, in Sept. 2015, the government made amendments to the security bill, finally allowing JSDF to use arms in its missions to rescue the Japanese living on foreign land.

† In the 1970s and 1980s, North Korean government agents abducted Japanese citizens from Japan, 17 of which are officially recognized by the Japanese government. Many more are missing; they are believed to have been abducted. In 2002, North Korea finally admitted and apologized for these abductions, but some of the victims have not returned to Japan, even to this day.

should have taken similar measures, but there were no signs of any such action. This shows that although the Abe administration was trying hard to change the Constitution of Japan at the time, its behavior was no different from those who had been opposing its alteration [Note: this is referring to the fact that the Abe administration could not think outside of the conventional interpretation of Article 9 and could not make the decision to rescue the Japanese living abroad.].

In the international community, messages are Only effective if they contain a value judgment

As for the hostage crisis, the Japanese government should have thought in a more logical manner. In fact, capturing people and demanding a ransom while threatening to kill them is something that barbaric thieves in a folk tale would do. Such behavior shall not be tolerated. Of course, some cultural characteristics had to be taken into account, but even so, the government had to make a value judgment; it should not have ended with the government simply begging for the hostages' lives.

At the very least, as a prime minister, Mr. Abe should have said to the Islamic State, "What you are doing is wrong. Should you execute the Japanese hostages, Japan shall regard the Islamic State as an enemy and take action accordingly while strengthening our ties with other countries." In other words, he should have said that executing the hostages would be taken as a declaration of war. In the international community, messages are only effective if they contain a value judgment. But his message was ambiguous, so people had no idea what he was trying to say.

Putting human lives first is the Japanese creed, As stated by Shichihei Yamamoto

It is the typical creed of the Japanese to put human lives first; they believe, ultimately, that human lives must be the highest priority.* The Japanese critic Shichihei Yamamoto, otherwise known as Isaiah Ben-Dasan, pointed this out. In Japan, there is a particular belief in the importance of putting human lives first.†

On the other hand, monotheistic religions such as Islam, Judaism and Christianity do not always place top priority on human life. In monotheistic religions, people believe that God comes before humans, and therefore God has the right to punish or reward human beings. So, they believe that God praises people when they have acted correctly, but punishes them when they have done wrong deeds.

This kind of thinking does not exist in the Japanese creed. Japanese people believe that securing human lives is a universal principle common to all countries. America does make efforts in human rights diplomacy, of course, but it is worthy to note that in monotheistic countries, there is a general belief that God exists above humans.

In fact, only Japan has a different belief on this point. Japan must say what must be said, rather than trying to resolve a problem just by using money.

Prime Minister Abe distributed money in the Middle East as humanitarian aid and used it as a condition to cooperate in releasing the

---

* Japanese people believe protecting human lives is of primary importance, because they believe there is no higher value than that. As opposed to the Western military that fight to protect, for example, freedom of speech or democracy, Japanese people are concerned with the loss of the soldiers' lives. That is why they have resistance against military forces and tend to be attached to the idea of pacifism.

† In his spiritual messages, too, recorded on May 29, 2013, Shichihei Yamamoto said that securing human lives is the core belief of what he calls *Nihonkyo*, or the Japanese creed. Refer to Ryuho Okawa, *Yamamoto Shichihei no Shin-Nihonjin-Ron* [The New Perspective on Japanese People by Shichihei Yamamoto](Tokyo: IRH Press, 2013).

hostages. I believe this was a good strategy. But he should have gone a step further and announced his strong conviction that he was assisting other countries because the Islamic State was committing wrong.

The only way to assess Whether something is right or wrong

It is very hard to judge whether something is right or wrong. There is only one way to assess this. That is to imagine what will happen if that course of action is pursued through to the end.

For example, it is not easy to judge whether the Islamic State's ambitions are just. However, just imagine what would happen if they expanded to the entire Islamic world and even further to Africa and Southern Europe. They intend to create a vast empire like the Ottoman Empire in the past. Do you think the expansion of a state, based on that mindset, would bring happiness to humanity? If you consider this and determine that it would bring humanity more misery than now, you must make a decision that the Islamic State's deeds are wrong. There is nothing wrong if its expansion means an expansion of happiness, but if not, you have to decide that what the Islamic State is doing is wrong.

I am saying the same thing in regard to China. In mainland China, everything is controlled by the will of President Xi Jinping, but in 2014, the Umbrella Revolution occurred in Hong Kong and people protested against the Chinese government by carrying yellow umbrellas. What would happen if China's ways of thinking were to spread throughout the world? When considering this, we can clearly see that an increasing number of nations and people would be unhappy. That is why I am against the expansion of China's way of thinking.

This is one approach. We can imagine whether a system would generate good or not when other people follow and spread it. It is important to judge whether it is good or evil based on this.

Ever since the American military abandoned Its role as the world's policeman, Chaos increased around the globe

President Obama won the Nobel Peace Prize for the military withdrawal in the Middle East, but this resulted in confusion there, creating many sources of instability in the area. Actually, there are two facets of military affairs; one is that it serves the role of police, and the other is that it functions as a brutal force such as the massacre of people. We need to be aware that ever since the American military abandoned its role of policeman, chaos, disorder and the number of deaths have increased around the world.

America is only conducting air strikes now. President Obama is unwilling to commit ground troops because that would endanger the lives of many Americans. That is why he only permits air strikes. However, from the point of view of the Islamic State, they probably see this as unfair because America is unilaterally attacking it using weapons that it does not possess.* Thus, we can say that America's Middle East policies contributed to the problem of the Islamic State.

Throughout the world, there is a tug-of-war going on between "the justice decided by God" and "the justice thought up by human

---

* The death toll on the Islamic State side caused by American air strikes is said to exceed 6,000. And on November 13, 2015, more terrorist attacks by the Islamic State occurred in multiple locations in France, including a concert hall and a restaurant in Paris, and a stadium in a nearby city, killing about 130 people and injuring more than 300 others. In retaliation for these attacks, the Western countries intensified their air attacks on Syria. It is reported that the Russian air strikes alone have killed more than 1,300 people, including about 400 civilians.

beings." This is the view regarding justice as seen from the perspective of religion. Please know this.

ᵥ✐ 4 ᵥ✐

WHAT IS RIGHTEOUSNESS IN TERMS OF ECONOMICS?

Provide people equality of opportunity, Rather than equality of outcome

There is also justice that involves economic issues. At the start of 2015, I spoke about the French economist Thomas Piketty.* He wrote *Capital in the Twenty-First Century,* a contemporary version of *Das Kapital,* and put forward the idea that the world would be better if wealth was distributed evenly by increasing progressive taxation on income and levying huge inheritance taxes. This is exactly the same thing Marx wrote in *The Communist Manifesto.* But I would like you to know that there are some problems with this way of thinking, so you need to give it careful consideration.

Let me explain this simply, using Japanese sumo wrestling as an example. In January 2015, Hakuho, a grand champion, or *yokozuna,* won the championship at the New Year Grand Sumo Tournament, marking a record number of tournament championships. He is now the only sumo wrestler to have won 33 tournaments.

With regard to this, there may be people who would be offended by his number of wins, thinking that this is unfair and not forgivable

---

* Refer to a lecture entitled, "A Lecture on *The Laws of Wisdom,*" given on January 11, 2015.

from the perspective of equality of outcome. They may say, "There is no need for one person to win 33 times, winning just once is enough. Once someone has won a championship, he has no right to win again; the victory should go to the next runner-up. If the wrestlers took turns winning the tournaments this way, there would have been 33 winners so far. This is what equality means." This is how seekers of equal outcome basically think.

However, you will easily see that there is something odd with this kind of thinking. Producing 33 winners who are happy to have achieved a tournament championship might seem beneficial to humanity, but something is not right about it. The odd part is that it does not fairly judge factors such as the effort and discipline a person has put in, or the happiness he has brought to many others. This kind of world is not right.

This would be the same as saying that the professional baseball player Ichiro gets too many hits and imposing restrictions on him by limiting the number of hits. There is definitely something wrong with this. Or, it would be the same as saying that part of his salary should be distributed to second-string players, since the salaries available to them would be diminished if he earns so much.

It is fine to distribute money to a certain degree as welfare benefits, but if everything were regulated by this kind of thinking, all sports including baseball and sumo wrestling would be boring. Apart from sports, in the world of business too, people are actually competing vigorously; they try hard to come up with better ideas and work very hard to survive.

Providing equal opportunity is extremely important and must be protected by law as well. However, as for outcomes, there will naturally be some disparity. While it is necessary to make the utmost effort to protect people in the worst situations, we need to accept that gaps will naturally emerge to a certain extent, and have a mind that is happy for others' success. Otherwise, the world will not progress overall. This is something that we need to know. Unless we know this, there will be various problems.

Make the spirit of noblesse oblige *a kind of culture*

There is an actress, aged about 20, who earns more than two million dollars a year. On hearing this, some people may think it is truly outrageous that a person can earn that kind of money at such a young age and that she should just keep one hundred thousand and give the rest to other people. However, it is extremely difficult to be able to earn so much money. She gained prominence and was highly recognized by many and won out in a highly competitive world. It is to attain this type of fame, that so many people aim to become actresses or celebrities. This is an undeniable fact.

To return to the example of the sumo wrestler, if people insist that Hakuho should not win because he is Mongolian and not Japanese, then this is certainly discrimination. There is no equality in that kind of situation and therefore not good. It is also not right to handicap him saying that five wins will be subtracted out of his total wins just because he is Mongolian.

Decades ago, the sumo wrestler Konishiki, originally from Hawaii, failed to become a grand champion, despite having achieved a fairly good record. At that time, some American papers complained one of which was *The New York Times*. It ran an article saying that Konishiki was not promoted to yokozuna due to racial discrimination. But in the tournament after the article was written, Konishiki gave a poor performance and his prospect for promotion faded away.

On the other hand, another Hawaiian-born sumo wrestler, Akebono, did become a yokozuna, and Mongolian-born Hakuho was not discriminated against either. This shows there is equality of opportunity. Whether a wrestler is Mongolian or any other nationality, those who have won several tournaments and achieved good results have been promoted to yokozuna rank properly.

It is natural that disparity emerges in results. This is unavoidable. Unless the winner is celebrated, the whole tournament would not be exciting and sumo wrestling itself would lose popularity and disappear. Therefore, we need to have both perspectives and know that a good balance between equality and disparity will lead to progress. Although some adjustments must be made, it is not good, just to make every outcome even and equal.

When Hakuho wins a tournament, he receives many envelopes containing prize money. Upon returning to his dressing room, he distributes the prize money to the group of attendants around him, such as those who follow him into the ring carrying a sword, bring him water, change his loincloths or wash him down when taking a bath. He shares the prize money with these people.

This act by him is what Happy Science calls "noblesse oblige," or the spirit of chivalry. As a yokozuna, he distributes the large sum of money he receives. There is nothing wrong in sharing the money with people whom he feels grateful for the work they have done for him. However, if all his prize money is forcefully taken from him and distributed to other people, he would lose motivation to win tournaments. That is why Happy Science puts great importance on having the spirit of noblesse oblige. We need to establish this attitude as a kind of culture.

It is essential to provide people with equal opportunity for achieving success, by widely opening the doors to success to as many people as possible and giving them chances. But in terms of results, a gap will naturally arise between people. This is a principle of capitalism. If this gap becomes too big and some people profit too much, then it is necessary to encourage them in a religious manner to use their wealth for social welfare to benefit many people. It goes without saying that various organizations, including national and local government bodies and non-profit organizations, should make efforts to extend assistance to people suffering without the aid of legal protection.

ℐ 5 ℒ

SPREAD THE THINKING OF PROGRESS AND PROSPERITY FROM JAPAN TO THE WORLD

Eliminating disparity will not do any good
Unless you use wisdom

As I have described in this chapter, there are two kinds of righteousness: one which is politically right and one which is economically right.

American political philosopher John Rawls [1921–2002] is famous for writing, *A Theory of Justice*. In this book he basically argues that justice means to eliminate disparity. In current terms, he says it is unforgivable that a mere one percent or so of the world's population possesses half of the world's wealth, and therefore it is essential to transfer the wealth of this one percent to other people.

However, the world's population is increasing rapidly, so even if the wealth were to be distributed, it would be diluted. Ultimately, it would only have as little effect as pouring wine into a river. This is the reality, so we need to use wealth wisely. For this reason, I do not think that simply eliminating disparity accords with justice. Eliminating disparity will not do any good unless you use wisdom.

I do believe it is important to keep offering assistance and opportunities to people who can rebound with some kind of support. Nevertheless, if we create a society that treats people in the same way regardless of how much or little they work, in other words, a society based on the ideals of communism, then that would be the end of humanity.

Teach how to fish, rather than giving fish

This chapter may have been philosophical and a little difficult to understand. I intend to create a new way of thinking that would spread from Japan to the world. I want to create logical and consistent principles on the issue of "righteousness," and on this basis, export ways of thinking that will bring about progress and prosperity.

Basically, I believe that teaching people how to fish, rather than giving them fish, is the right approach. If you give people fish, they will eventually consume it, but if you teach them how to fish, they will be able to catch their own fish all through their life.

Japan can contribute to the world in this way. Yet, Japanese people must reflect deeply on the fact that their idea of justice lacks value judgments in the religious sense.

Chapter 4

The
PRINCIPLE
of
JUSTICE

Ways of Thinking Regarding
"Justice on a Personal Level"
And "Justice Between Nations"

ℐ 1 ℣

JUSTICE:
THE MOST DIFFICULT TOPIC OF OUR DAY

Justice on a personal level
Is mostly determined by the law

This chapter will discuss the theme, "The Principle of Justice." In the 1980s, I presented teachings on different themes in the "Principles Series."* But I have yet to speak clearly on the principle of justice, which is, in a sense, the most difficult issue we face today.

Upon reading the front page of a newspaper, watching the news on a major television network or hearing all kinds of comments and opinions, it is truly hard to give an exact answer to the question, "What is the ideal form of justice in today's world?" Strictly speaking, the justice in connection to our individual lives is generally determined by the rule of law. We usually live abiding by the law and decide justice based on whether something conforms to the law.

Today, criminal law and civil law cover many of the rules that have been given in God's teachings in old religions. For example, on a personal level, the commandment, "You shall not kill" could be interpreted into modern criminal law as the law against homicide, which comes with severe penalties if violated. The commandment, "You shall not steal" could be the law against theft, which also comes with punishment if violated. As you can see, the old commandments are incorporated in modern criminal law.

---

* These are published as *The Science of Happiness: 10 Principles for Manifesting Your Divine Nature* (Vermont: Destiny Books, 2009).

Civil law deals with disputes between individuals and tries to resolve problems with money. For instance, when disputes arise concerning land ownership, such as the boundary line between two properties, the court will intervene and settle the dispute according to the law.

When it comes to marriage, although it is primarily an invisible contract between two individuals, the law provides legality. It can also dissolve marriage and allow divorce. Therefore, although marriage and divorce are merely about signing a contract, they are based on the law and are bound by it.

In this way, on a daily level, laws passed from bills proposed by legislators, elected by a majority of the people, rule the everyday lives of the citizens. And when those laws no longer reflect the will of society, they will take measures such as making new laws to deal with them.

Having said this, there are differences between nations; an activity can be considered a crime in one country, but not a crime in another. For example, while some countries have started to legalize same-sex marriage, there are also countries that do not legally recognize this. Or, while some countries strictly control narcotics and stimulants, others are much more lenient.

These are very difficult issues. While we could let the law decide what is right and what is wrong, there are actually differences between countries or regions. In countries like the U.S., there are differences, even from state to state, and the country does not necessarily take a unified stance on certain issues. Nevertheless, we could say that in general, justice is mostly determined by law.

Religious themes are at the basis of justice
On the issue of denuclearizing the Middle East

When a problem surpasses the individual level and becomes a much larger one, the situation evolves into a clash of value systems. That is to say, it becomes a conflict between companies, between organizations or between countries. This has been the seed of different kinds of disputes sprouting around the world.

Let's go back to May 2015. A discussion took place in the U.N. regarding the abolition of nuclear weapons for Middle Eastern countries. However, the discussion dissipated before it came to any conclusion because of opposition from countries such as the United States and the United Kingdom.

We all know that Israel has nuclear arms. Israel, with its small population of just under 10 million people, has nuclear capability, whereas the surrounding Islamic nations with far greater populations are not allowed to do the same. Where exactly does justice lie in that? The answer is extremely ambiguous.

It is understandable that the U.S. and the U.K. support Israel and accept its possession of nuclear arms to prevent Israel from being crushed. If we seek to uncover the basis of that position, we would find that it involves religious themes.

People in Christian nations all over the world read not only the New Testament, but also the Old Testament. The Old Testament contains the history of the nation of Israel and the teachings of the numerous messiahs and prophets from that region. People in Christian nations study these, so they strongly feel that they must preserve the nation of Israel and protect the teachings of God in the Old Testament.

On the other hand, how do they regard Islam, which arose after

Christianity? It is not that they do not recognize Islamic countries as valid societies or states. However, deep in their hearts, they strongly retain a belief that, from the perspective of their religious principles, Islam is a collection of evil teachings that are outdated.

Of course, they do not say it outright. If they were to say that Islam represents the teachings of the devil, Muslims would get furious. Perhaps that would lead to more threats of multiple terrorist incidents. Thus, it is something people cannot speak openly, not only in Japan, but in Christian nations, too. In reality, there has been no decisive winner in the conflict between the Christian civilization and the Islamic civilization, despite having fought three large wars during the Crusades. Hostility continues to this day.

From the viewpoint of the Christian civilization, the Islamic world seems like a place where terrorism is rampant. Therefore, in order to suppress the roots of that terrorism, they believe they must not allow Islamic nations to obtain immense power. They think, "If we let Islamic countries have nuclear weapons, what would we do when they commit terrorism with those nuclear weapons?" That is why the U.S. and the U.K. are pushing the idea that it is acceptable for Israel to have nuclear weapons, but not the Islamic nations.

However, this idea obviously comes from a sort of value judgment; a cultural value judgment definitely influences it. Of course, it is debatable whether such judgment is right or not.

In reality, Israel is in a position where it could easily annihilate several hundred million surrounding Muslims, but if these Muslims were to attack Israel, they would immediately suffer a nuclear attack. Thus, we can also say that the Western approach is quite one-sided.

Was there justice
In the persecution of the Jewish people?

There is yet another perspective. For example, in World War II, the Jewish people suffered severe persecution at the hands of Hitler. It is said that some six million Jews were executed in concentration camps such as Auschwitz. It was a horrible tragedy.

For the background of this occurrence, we have to go all the way back to the time when Jesus was executed in approximately 30 AD. Some 40 years after that, the Land of Judea ceased to exist and the Jewish people were put under Roman rule. Then, they scattered all over the world for some 1,900 years, without having their own nation of Israel. These people have also been called the "Diaspora," meaning "a scattered people." They wandered about as a people without country for 1,900 years.

In addition, in the medieval period, the Jewish people were not well liked because of their practice of lending money as a business. This is a well-known fact that even appears in one of Shakespeare's plays. Jewish people believed that money and diamonds were the only things that they could fall back on; they were inclined toward finance. That is why they were not so well liked. Therefore, negative feelings toward the Jewish people had already existed in medieval Europe in the backdrop of the behavior of Hitler in the modern world.

Furthermore, there is the following account in the New Testament. When Jesus was sent to be nailed to the cross, there was a particularly brutal criminal among those designated for execution. The Roman governor pronounced that he would pardon either this man or Jesus, and asked the populace to decide. The Jewish people gathered in an atrium, with the priests taking the lead, and proclaimed with force that they wanted the Roman government to execute Jesus and set the murderer free with a judgment of not guilty. They also said that they and their descendants would bear the responsibility for this. This is spelled out clearly in the New Testament, so if someone were to say, "That curse was fulfilled two thousand years later," it could not be fully denied.

Things are determined over the long span of history, so this is an extremely difficult topic. You could say that the descendants of the Jewish people are now being asked to atone for their ancestors' sin of executing Jesus, two thousand years later. By declaring, "Place the price for that blood upon us," the Jewish people at the time put responsibility of the execution of Jesus on Israel, not Rome. Thus, saying that Hitler took advantage of this fact to fulfill his ambition could be one interpretation, too.*

Determining justice concerning Ongoing problems is a very difficult thing to do

With these circumstances, after World War II, there was a consensus to create a country for the Jewish people in order to compensate for the atrocities they suffered. Thus, the nation of Israel was established by partitioning a section of the Middle East by the power of the West. However, this gave rise to various disputes with Arabic nations, yielding consecutive wars in the Middle East.

What would happen if there was a sympathetic view to justify the Jewish people's ability to defend themselves? One could say, for example, "Jewish people suffered in war at the hands of the Hitler regime,

---

* The author is not approving the Jewish Holocaust. According to his spiritual investigation, the spirit of Hitler has fallen and become a devil in Hell. See Ryuho Okawa, *The Golden Laws: History through the Eyes of the Eternal Buddha* (Tokyo: HS Press, 2015).

so it is only natural that they get their own country. It is only natural that they receive special treatment and be given nuclear weapons to arm and protect themselves."

If you follow that same logic, you could say the same thing about Japan. Japan is the only nation on which atomic bombs were dropped in World War II. Only Japan had suffered the fallout from atomic bombs twice. So, by following the same logic, you could arrive at a conclusion that states, "Japan lost two hundred thousand lives in a mere instant through the monstrous act of dropping atomic bombs. That was inhuman. Thus, Japan is the only nation that should be allowed to have nuclear arms, since it suffered damage from the atomic bombs, and should be pitied." This is a valid direction to think in if you follow the same logic used in the case of Israel, though we cannot go that far at this time.

The Germans still live in penance for what they did because they invaded Europe under Hitler's regime. Nevertheless, it is an undeniable fact that the current EU is centered around Germany. In other words, the core nation of the EU is "a country that is atoning."

On the other hand, looking at the Pacific region, Japan, a nation that is constantly apologizing, is at the core. Countries in Asia and Oceania are trembling in fear of the current Chinese hegemony, so they are relying on Japan. They are hoping that Japan can serve as some sort of shield against China.

For this reason, Prime Minister Abe has decided to support islands in the Pacific Ocean with a total of 55 billion yen [approx. 450 million dollars] to maintain friendly alliances. Put bluntly, he is moving in the direction of enabling self-defense. That is to say, he is setting up a way of countering China's Maritime Silk Road Initiative with "island-based self-protection." This may appear similar to the Greater East

Asia Co-Prosperity Sphere idea that Japan set up before the Greater East Asia War, but he is doing so because he senses the danger.

In this way, when the issue of justice is viewed on a grand scale, it becomes extremely confusing. Also, historically justice has been determined when historians look back on events and make judgments. Therefore, it is very difficult to make value judgments on current events or to make value judgments in advance concerning upcoming events.

✑ 2 ✒

JUSTICE SEEN FROM THE STANDPOINT OF RELIGION

Justice on a personal level starts from An awareness as a child of God, or a child of Buddha

My intention in this chapter is to discuss the issue of justice, starting from "justice on a personal level" and then "justice between nations." If I were to speak of this theme from the standpoint of religion, I must first address the question, "What is justice on a personal level?"

As I wrote in my book entitled *Shin Nihonkoku Kenpo Shian* [Draft Proposal for a New Constitution of Japan] (Tokyo: IRH Press, 2009), I believe that justice is realized when each individual is allowed to move in the direction of achieving his or her own self-realization and, by doing so, develop a deeper awareness as a child of God or a child of Buddha. Therefore, I could conversely say that any movement that suppresses this is wrong.

Materialistic research has seeped much into school education, universities and society, also heavily infiltrating the field of science. Obviously, there are some useful effects from it. For example, it is no doubt true that the bullet train and maglev lines would not have progressed this far without materialistic research. I do not mean to reject those things, of course.

However, I must say people are definitely being misled if accepting those things are leading them to reject spiritual matters, the other world, God and Buddha, by a simple attitude of determining whether something is "black or white" or "yes or no." This means that an obvious mistake is infiltrating modern school education, university-level education and the scientific activities of professionals.

People's philosophies and creed become stained as they conduct research or make a living within this flow of mistaken education; they will gradually lose awareness as children of God or children of Buddha. They will even think that human life is an existence limited only to this world. This is very frightening.

Therefore, seen from a personal level, any movement that deprives people of awareness as a child of God or a child of Buddha is a hindrance in realizing justice. The right action is to create a social system that allows people to be aware that they are spiritual beings endowed with souls while living in physical bodies, that there are high spirits, God and Buddha in the heavenly world and that they are children of God and Buddha.

Modern political doctrine started from The denial of the Manichaean dualism of good and evil

Taking the point even further, this hindrance has to do with modern political doctrine. Put simply, the mistake started from the philoso-

106

phy of Immanuel Kant.

Kant's philosophy contains concepts that come under the category of ideas of justice. The German philosopher rejected the Manichaean dualism of good and evil, and advocated "maxims," subjective principles of action based on reason. He put forth the "categorical imperative," a concept which suggests that one should choose to live, of one's own will, in a way which one believes will accord with morality. In other words, his suggestion was this: "Set aside the concept of good and evil determined by God and, regarding actions you take based on reason, carry them out in a way that would be acceptable if other people did the same thing. This is the new way of determining justice."

This way of thinking is quite easy to understand in a "Godless age." Having that way of thinking, Kant clearly rejected the Manichaean dualism of good and evil. However, such dualism was not limited to Manichaeism alone.

It is a fact that Christianity conflicted with Manichaeism. While Christianity started in the first century of the Christian era, Manichaeism became active from around 200 to 300 AD. Manichaeism grew to the level of a world religion for a time even as its founder was still alive. However, it was immensely persecuted by Christianity, and was ultimately annihilated by Persian Zoroastrianism, which was the base of Manichaeism.

Incidentally, in *Confessions*, Saint Augustine wrote on the theme of converting from this kind of Manichaean thought back to Christianity. I believe that Kant's way of thinking was based on this book.

Yet, the dualistic way of thinking of good and evil advocated by Manichaeism is also seen in many other religions. Buddhism also teaches good and evil, as does Christianity. Various religions contain the idea of good and evil.

Basically, religions that do not teach good and evil are extremely rare. Some sects of Zen Buddhism or the True Pure Land school of Buddhism may state that good and evil can no longer be separated, that it is all one, but they are saying this in a completely different context. It does not mean that good and evil are not existent. Promoting the good and suppressing the bad in people is one of the Buddha's fundamental philosophies and, from a religious perspective, this is the way it has to be.

So, Kant rejected the teachings that came from God or Buddha in the heavenly world and thought that justice conforms to doing what other people can follow. He considered that an individual's acts based on his or her own will in the world of human beings would become a maxim or a subjective principle that would influence other people. This became the starting point of the modern era.

Furthermore, the ideology of social contract theory by thinkers such as John Locke [1632–1704] and Jean-Jacques Rousseau [1712–1778] also came into play. People began to hold the idea that creating a social contract and binding people's lives to it are the right direction. In other words, modern society tried to create a society that did not need God or Buddha.

How did modern political reform arise?

Thus, there was a trend where people wanted to shift away from the church. This is probably due to factors such as the heresy trials of the medieval period, religious conflicts between Protestants and Catholics and various confusions caused by the intervention of churches. To put it another way, philosophy and science began to separate from religion, with the intention of moving away from the church. Kant must have been fully aware of that. He must have known that his attempt was to "decapitate God."

Then, the French Revolution occurred. The French Revolution was sparked by the ideas of thinkers like Kant and Rousseau and was a major thrust in modern political reform. Many good things came from this, of course. Equality and freedom were promoted. Individuals were recognized as independent entities and they were able to act as constituent citizens of their nation-state or as individual subjects with the right of sovereignty. Compared to the past, the responsibilities, obligations, abilities, authority, and rights ascribed to the individual grew immensely. In this sense, there were good aspects of reform. On the other hand, there were also elements that were forgotten and left behind. I feel that these became the next major problem.

Today, "warm-hearted justice" is disappearing

Modern philosophy no longer understands God or Buddha. Similarly, in the field of science, there is a fundamental principle that denies any world that cannot be seen with the naked eye. This has continued for two to three hundred years now. Due to this, religion is now being treated as a subject similar to cultural anthropology and archaeology.

Simply put, religious studies is now considered to be on the same level as, for example, digging up things like human bones, vessels, sarcophagi and stone axes, with commentary like, "Let's look at this from an archaeological viewpoint" or "How did these people live in terms of cultural anthropology?" People today often think that there is no need to look back to 2,000-year old philosophies because they think that they are the most advanced and that ancient people were primitive in every way.

However, the philosophy of the 20th and 21st centuries that modern people believe are much advanced has not actually developed since the era of Socrates and Plato some two thousand years ago. It has merely transformed into theoretical matter, like playing word games, becoming symbols and mathematics. Thus, it has become something completely severed from people's way of life. From this, we cannot necessarily say that we have actually advanced. This is why I have the impression that "warm-hearted justice" is being lost.

ℰ 3 ℒ

HOW TO CONSIDER JUSTICE IN DEBATES OVER THE CONSTITUTION OF JAPAN

Scholars' misinterpretation of constitutionalism

In 2015, the left-wing groups in Japan had been regaining power as shown in the movement opposing the relocation of a U.S. military base within Okinawa Prefecture from Futenma to Henoko, which was also supported by the prefectural governor. Included in the debate were issues that emphasized the Constitution of Japan. The objections mainly centered on the issue of Article 9 of the constitution.

Japan renounced war in Article 9 of its constitution. In other words, Japan can no longer engage in war. It also abolished land, sea and air forces. This means that Japan has abandoned war as a method to resolve international disputes. In actuality, however, there is an amazingly large contradiction here.

Regarding this issue, everyone enthusiastically advocates constitutionalism, particularly constitutional scholars as well as the typical professional left wing journalists that appear in newspapers and television. What they are saying is this: "The emperor, prime minister, other ministers, officials and civil servants are all bound by constitutionalism. However, now there are many laws being passed based on the current administration's interpretation of the constitution, including security-related laws. This is not right."

Regarding this, it could be difficult to understand if I were to explain it in too much detail, since not all readers are experts in the law. So, I would like to point out the error in their line of thought in the simplest possible terms.

The constitution does not bind the people; The sovereign people create the constitution

Then, where is the error? Constitutionalism essentially means creating a constitution and its associated laws and carrying out the politics of the nation based on these. There is also "constitutional monarchy" which, as the term suggests, maintains a system of monarchy while adhering to a constitution. In other words, since monarchs can easily transform into dictators, in the case of a constitutional monarchy, the function of the monarch is defined to a certain extent in the constitution. The limits of what the monarch can and cannot do are clearly specified.

The Constitution of Japan also has that aspect to some degree. It states that the emperor shall not have powers related to government. The emperor's acts in matters of state are also clearly defined; he is unable to do anything other than those specific things. This shows that the Constitution of Japan is, at least in part, a constitution that binds the monarch in a constitutional monarchy style.

The word "constitutionalism" in and of itself does not mean more than "establishing a constitution." It is purely limited to the idea of "establishing a constitution and running a country based on it." There is also the term, "constitutional democracy," which means "democracy based on an established constitution." Some countries adopt this system. Among the democratic nations, there are constitutional democracies based on an established constitution.

Then, in a constitutional democracy, can a constitution restrict democracy? The generally accepted answer is, "No, it cannot restrict democracy." The reason is that the Constitution of Japan includes the notion of the sovereignty of the people. The people are sovereign and, as an expression of their sovereignty, they can create a constitution and laws. In other words, constitutions can be created through that kind of democratic willpower. Therefore, a constitution cannot completely restrict the very nature of democracy itself.

Constitutional scholars are confusing Constitutionalism with rule of law

Constitutionalism is often mistaken for "rule of law." Scholars tend to confuse constitutionalism with the rule of law, in which every single matter is thought of in terms of the law as a base. They often take constitutionalism to mean "rule by the constitution," which leads them to the conclusion that the constitution rules over everything. Even constitutional scholars, who are the experts in this field, tend to use the word "constitutionalism" in the same way as "rule of law," but there is a great error in this.

A constitution determines the general direction of a nation and its attitude. Basically, it is composed of a section that protects fundamental human rights and a section that defines the framework of the nation. As far as the framework is concerned, most constitutions set forth the separation of powers into three branches of government: legislative, executive and judicial. So, put simply, a constitution is made up of a section that protects the rights of the people and a section that outlines the principles of the government.

However, because the wording is abstract with a small number of articles, the constitution cannot get into specifics. Because of this, a constitution naturally needs to have interpretations added depending on the times and necessity, or be given a more concrete shape by adding new laws. In this way, its meanings must be altered little by little as time goes on. I believe this is the area where constitutional scholars do not understand.

Japanese scholars tend to think that, just like the "Ten Commandments of Moses," the constitution must be preserved for ages to come once it has been set. However, in reality, this is not the case; there is room for interpretation. Thus, I must say that it is basically wrong to think that the constitution must never be adjusted.

The very Constitution of Japan itself is unconstitutional

Those who are against the revision of the constitution, in particular, do not understand the concept of sovereignty. This is where the problem lies. Fundamentally speaking, they have no concept of sovereignty.

In fact, the current Constitution of Japan in and of itself is actually unconstitutional. In other words, Article 9 of the constitution does not allow Japan to maintain land, sea, or air forces, nor use war as a method of resolving international disputes. So, if you read this straightforwardly, it is written that in the country of Japan, its sovereign people cannot protect themselves even if they wanted to do so.

Put directly, Article 9 itself violates the sovereignty of the people, but the people who are against revising the constitution do not see that. There is a clear aspect of the constitution that contradicts the way a sovereign nation thinks. They must think deeply about this.

Thus, currently, the left-wing people in Japan often mention "constitutionalism" and the words "constitutionalism" and "left wing" have been used almost interchangeably, but that is a mistake. The word "constitutionalism" means to run a nation based on a constitution, which is not the same as "rule of law."

℘ 4 ℘

THE DANGERS OF NOMOCRACY AND RULE OF LAW

The opposite of nomocracy is "governance by virtue"

Rule of law is an approach that is very close to the ideology of nomocracy [a system of government based on a legal code]. Some people believe that nomocracy and a nation ruled by law are good things. Nomocracy is actually the idea that says, "We are governed by the law."

This is very similar to normal rules at school. Even though the school regulations dictate specific matters, all sorts of individual problems occur. Therefore, the principal, the vice principal and the teachers have to add their own judgment for each specific case. In other words, they sometimes need to judge whether a specific behavior violates school regulations. Similarly, nomocracy is not completely almighty because in reality, you cannot bind everything with the law.

Speaking on this further, "nomocracy" was created as a word opposing the idea of "rule by virtue." It came about as a concept to refute "governance by virtue." I often teach that rule by virtue is very important. At the beginning of the seventh century in Japan, Prince Shotoku enacted the Seventeen-Article Constitution.* Some scholars criticize that it cannot be considered a constitution or a law because it is based on rule by virtue. However, in the modern era as well, we could say that President Lincoln ruled by virtue. Furthermore, the Constitution of the United States of America includes the concept, "mission as humans created by God," which shows the element of rule by virtue.

Consider what would happen if a leader with only a superficial understanding of humans were to appear. He would feel he could rule the world and regulate people's lifestyle solely by the power of reason that controls mechanized civilization and robots. Unfortunately, in that case, society would be cold-hearted.

Nomocracy can get dangerous if taken too far

Nomocracy is fine in general. Just like traffic regulations, the rules apply equally to everyone. Applying them differently to certain people would cause trouble. However, if nomocracy is not enforced with care, it can actually result in constraining people, making them incompetent and unhappy. Finding this balance is a very difficult thing to do.

---

* Prince Shotoku [574–622] was a regent under Empress Suiko. He created the basis of a centralized government in Japan. The Seventeen-Article Constitution he advocated in 604 AD contained the spirit of government by virtue, which was based on Buddhism and Confucianism.

For example, Chinese President Xi Jinping believes in legalism, which is an idea that says established laws are almighty and people should be ruled by them. Apparently, he is currently basing his leadership of China on the model of Han Fei [280–233 BC], the man who wrote the book *Han Feizi*, and Shang Yang [390–338 BC], the leader who established a nation based on legalism.

However, Shang Yang wound up being executed under the very laws that he established. There was more weight given to the law than the lawmaker and the very lawmaker was killed based on his own laws. In the late 19th and early 20th centuries, a similar case occurred in Japan. These things can happen, so we must be careful of this type of extreme thinking.

This sort of problem can happen when a dictator makes the laws, but it can also happen even when people make laws as sovereign entities. It would be disastrous if all people were killed for breaking the law that they had created themselves. If there is danger of that happening, the law itself should be changed instead. This is why nomocracy should not be taken too far.

Creating more laws to restrict freedom Will lead to less convenient lives

In general, rule by law is fine. The best aspect of the law is that it provides people with warnings in advance, for example, "If you do this, it will be considered a crime" or "You will be fined." Or, in disputes with others concerning rights, you will be taught in advance, "According to civil law, you will lose if you do this." Hence, the law can be extremely helpful in preventing disputes.

However, you should not expect that everything works in this manner. Particularly in the legislature, new laws are enacted year after year. When compared to my student years, *The Complete Book of the Six Codes** has grown larger to a size that can no longer be carried around. It is so thick that it can no longer be read in full; it is like an encyclopedia. It is slightly concerning whether anyone can manage to memorize the entire thing.

Lots of laws are made in this way, so laws that are no longer needed must be weeded out. However, it is almost impossible to abolish them because they are not temporary legislation. For this reason, laws continue to increase without ever decreasing. This is a very serious matter. Just as I am always saying that less taxes are better, less laws are also better. That is because laws constrain human lives.

As economist Friedrich Hayek puts it, laws are like pillars that you cannot bump into. You are allowed to move freely as long as you stay away from them, in other words, as long as you live within the scope of the law. That is to say, laws as a means to secure freedom are fine, but creating more laws that simply restrict freedom will lead to less convenient lives, which is not good at all.

We cannot allow the law to live on And the people to die out

I am not rejecting the way the modern government is operating centering on the law. But it is also true that the law is not almighty. At the same time, while international law exists and international institutions may intervene in a case, it is also a fact that, without the guaranteed power to enforce the rules, there are actually countries that

---

* A book that contains the six major categories in Japanese law and its associated rules, a few of which are the Constitution of Japan, the criminal code and the civil code.

will not follow them. In this sense, there are times when countries must make a decision with courage.

The Abe administration submitted the safety and security-related bills to the legislature.* From the viewpoint of the left wing, these bills are the equivalent of "war bills." Therefore, they are trying to prevent these bills from passing by insisting that "due process" would be to revise Article 9 of the constitution first. What they are saying is correct as a logical argument. However, the government is attempting to set up legislation to establish a system that can protect the nation even in case they fail to revise the constitution.

The constitution is a part of Japan's structure of state, of course, but I believe that it is natural for the people, who are the foundation of legislative authority, to raise objections or make modifications regarding cases that virtually infringe on their lives, safety and property. This is something like "a right to revolt" or "a right to implement a national emergency."

Suppose something happened and everyone was forced into an Auschwitz-like concentration camp and was killed. There would clearly be something wrong if nothing could be done to prevent such an event. I believe it is wrong to let the law live on while the people die out. If justice is not realized and injustice prevails throughout the world, then some natural disaster may occur as a reaction.† But we must do all we can as human beings to prevent such situations.

Right now, China is starting to take a slightly conciliatory stance toward Japan, but their intention to invade foreign countries is obvious; they are attempting to occupy a coral reef in the Spratly Islands

---

* On September 19, 2015, the House of Councillors of Japan approved and passed the bills including permission to exercise the right of collective self-defense.

† Refer to Ryuho Okawa, *Dai-shinsai Yocho Reading* [Reading on the Signs of a Major Earthquake] (Tokyo: IRH Press, 2015).

by constructing a two-mile long airstrip there. If things keep going as they are now, a conflict will most probably arise. So, the U.S. is putting heavy restraints on this. That is why China has started to lean closer toward Japan. Some countries do not concede unless they sense some threat, so Japan should not just cling to its conventional ways of thinking.

Additionally, stopping what is aggressively evil is not against the will of the heavenly world. While an invasive attack is not acceptable, I believe that having deterrent forces for defensive purposes is needed at the present time* until humanity overcomes barbaric qualities.

ℰ 5 ℒ

HOW JUSTICE IS DEFINED IN THE WORLD

The two major trends opposing each other in the world

In fact, there are two major trends opposing each other in the world today. One centers around the United States. This force is comprised of countries that want to support and spread the ideologies of democracy, liberalism, fundamental human rights and market economies. The other is a force comprised of countries that will suffer if these ideologies spread across the world, because their ways of thinking and methods differ. There is a battle between these two forces.

---

* This chapter was written based on the author's lecture given on May 24, 2015 and this paragraph takes into account the political situation of Japan at the time. Japan's ruling party [the Liberal Democratic Party, LDP] submitted a security bill to the Diet of Japan on May 14, only 10 days prior to the lecture. The opposing parties strongly refuted against this bill, the mass media made numerous comments on it and the people held demonstrations. However, the Diet passed this bill in September, thus giving the JSDF less restrictions to defend Japan.

For example, some countries would not be happy if democracy was pushed upon them. Their names may contain the words like "democratic" or "people's republic," but those names do not reflect the reality of what is happening in those countries. North Korea and China claim to be democracies, but their form of government actually means that people could be executed at any time, which is terrible. A name without actions to accompany it is no good. What is more, these countries do not guarantee fundamental human rights.

The U.S. points this out, but it is also undergoing a "retaliation" of its own. Recently, there have been many incidents of shootings of black people and problems related to racism. So, Americans must also be repentant on this point.

Incidentally, when studying American international political science, I get the sense that Americans believe democratic countries do not make war of invasion. They may not be aware of what they are actually doing. In international political science, they teach that democratic nations do not commit war of invasion. In other words, they believe that the U.S. is just engaged in wars of self-defense, not of invasion, and see that wars of self-defense are occurring on a global scale. It seems that, according to their ways of thinking, being democratic means not committing war of invasion. Happy Science does not think American ways of thinking are always right, so we somehow need to encourage them to correct this point.

In the Islamic world, on the other hand, punishments are too strict for the actual crimes committed, as seen from the perspective of liberalism, democracy and the protection of fundamental human rights. There are cases where limbs are cut off, one after another, for each crime; the right hand, the left leg, and so on. There was also the case where a princess of an Islamic country fell in love in the U.K. and, after returning home, was partially buried in a hole and stoned to death. This kind of punishment is too severe. Her behavior may have gone against Islamic culture, but such punishments are too extreme. There is definitely a need for improvement in their interpretation of fundamental human rights.

Furthermore, regarding the market economy, even China and Russia are in the process of becoming market economies. This trend cannot be reversed.

Mistakes will occur unless people Recognize the world that transcends this world

Please be aware that right now, the trend centering around the U.S. and the trend opposing it are clashing against each other. Basically, I feel that going with the trend centering on the U.S. is the right direction and consider this to conform with justice. But at the same time, I must state that there is something lacking in this trend as well.

As I mentioned earlier, the ideas, "God and Buddha exist" and "Humans are spiritual beings endowed with a soul, which undergoes soul training in this world and originally lives in the other world called the Real World" are missing. If an idea that rejects these as illusions and superstitions of ancient times infiltrates into the mainstream mentality, that idea is mistaken.

For example, the attitude of only seeking happiness in this world may well lead to the idea of utilitarianism advocated by the British philosopher Jeremy Bentham [1748–1832]. Interestingly, in the Japanese translation of a book on Jeremy Bentham, I found the phrase "kofuku-no-kagaku," meaning "happy science." So, "Happy Science" existed in the past, not only in the present.

By "happy science," Bentham meant that happiness could be measured. Put simply, there is a calculation for the happiness in this world, and by using a formula of utility, it is possible to determine what must be done to achieve the greatest happiness of the greatest number of people. According to his idea, happy science means being able to calculate happiness and is an approach to increase the total amount of happiness in this world by using a mathematical formula.

However, this idea denies the existence of the other world. While it is good for this world to become a better place, mistakes will arise if you do not accept the world that transcends this world.

Eliminating economic disparities will kill freedom

Essentially, Bentham's utilitarian calculations mostly deal with political and economic matters. His ideas developed into a concept of "one-person one-vote" in the political arena and "correcting income inequality" in the economic arena.

For example, there is a view that states, "If you compare the wealth seized by the top ten percent of a country with the bottom ten percent, then in many places, you would see an economic disparity of about ten to one. Therefore, reducing this inequality accords with justice." Thomas Piketty holds this idea, as did the American political philosopher John Rawls [1921–2002], who wrote *A Theory of Justice*.

In reality, however, economic disparities cannot be completely eliminated. Eliminating disparities will kill freedom, so it is not possible to make them disappear completely. Of course, social welfare is needed to a certain extent. It is true that people need something that guarantees their basic right to survive or something that supports their subsistence.

On the international level, the disparity ratio in economic power can even be as large as one to one hundred. What would happen if people thought such disparity was unfair and Japan decided to accept one hundred million immigrants, roughly the equivalent of its population, from the poorest countries of the world? If it did, Japan would undoubtedly be thrown into chaos. To receive immigrants, it would need to conduct research in stages to consider their education standards and the kinds of jobs it could provide them; otherwise the economic level in Japan would suddenly decline. That is why this kind of research would be necessary.

Is the one-person one-vote parity really fair?

In terms of political elections, right now the international system is approaching a one-person one-vote parity. In a way, this may be considered the realization of equality, but whether or not this is truly fair is questionable.

To put this another way, be it a Nobel Prize winning scholar, a political science expert, or a job-hopping drifter, each individual has no more power than his or her own single vote in the one-person one-vote system. However, for some people, this is questionable.

For example, upper-bracket taxpayers who have to give half of their income in taxes may want to say that they deserve at least two votes. Their feelings are quite understandable from the perspective of fairness. They probably feel, "Some hundreds of thousands of dollars that I have paid are being used by the government. This waterworks project over here is being carried out using tax money that I paid, and those streets over there were built with my tax money as well. But because there is only one vote for each person, my vote only has as much weight as someone who doesn't even work at all. That is unfair." I can understand their feelings, and it is indeed questionable if the one-person one-vote system is truly fair. Nevertheless, in quantitative terms, it is "equal."

Economically speaking, if everything was made equal, it would result in a completely socialist economy, and a military dictatorship would be the only government that could possibly work with that system. Therefore, it would rarely work in practice.

Of course, it is important to support the bottom segment. However, if the support grows too large and people get used to receiving subsidies, an increasing number of people would not have any incentive to work, and the people at the top level would also lose motivation. As a result, the country as a whole would decline. That is not the right direction to head in. Therefore, it is vital to open the path for people who want to work hard and make progress.

On the other hand, it is necessary to provide a certain level of help to people in need of immediate aid, while at the same time encouraging them to get back on their own feet again. This is the desirable way. In that sense, we need to consider thoroughly how to provide people with the equality of opportunity. Yet, when it comes to the equality of outcome, it is nearly impossible to get rid of disparity, though too large of it would be a problem, too.

Without economic success, there would be no money available to make various investments. As a result, the overall economy would shrink and start to decline. This is what happened in the United Kingdom. The Labor Party grew powerful, causing the development of the country to slow drastically after World War II. After the end of World War I, Britain was still the strongest power in the world, but now in some areas, they are considered to be 50 years behind Japan.

The reason for this is very clear. After World War II, the government switched between the Labor Party and the Conservative Party, which destabilized its political framework and shrunk its economy. This is something that needs to be considered carefully.

"Justice on a personal level" and "justice for the whole"

Generally speaking, a world where people can work toward awakening as a child of God, or Buddha, is most desirable on a personal level. For the whole, on the other hand, it is important to create a society that allows people of various backgrounds, regardless of their level of development, to continue holding their dreams to create an ideal utopia.

MASS MEDIA'S "RIGHT TO SILENCE" WILL MISLEAD A COUNTRY

When it comes to media literacy,
One problem is the mass media's "right to silence."
Although no one is pointing this out
And it is not written in any textbooks
Or reference books,
The most crucial problem concerning the relationship
Between democratic society and mass media
Is the right to silence held by the mass media.

In other words, if they remain silent about something,
Then it virtually does not exist.
If the evening newspapers and TV stations
Show the images of a rally
Crying out against "war bills"
With people holding up signs to say so,
Then that march does indeed exist,

Giving the impression that
The citizens are against those bills,
Even if the rally were conducted
By a mere four hundred people.
On the other hand,
If TV and the newspapers do not cover
A rally conducted by several thousand people
Of the opposing side,
Then the rally virtually does not exist.
The mass media uses this right to silence
At their own discretion
Without being reviewed by anyone.
No one is really checking which mass media outlet
Has stayed silent and about which part.
This right to silence is actually a gigantic power.

For example, if you read several different newspapers,
You will see that the same topic is reported differently.
A topic may take up the entire front page in one paper,
While that topic may be mentioned slightly
On the back page of another.
Some other paper may even cover the topic a day late.
Thus, they use all sorts of techniques to report it.
Even for advertisements,
Some papers do not run a certain kind of ad,
While others alter it before they run it.
They do all sorts of things like that.
We need to do further research on media literacy.
Otherwise, the correct form of democracy,
Or a sound democracy, will not grow
And a country will be misled to its ruin.

From "The Principle of Justice" Q&A

Chapter 5

The GREAT TURNING POINT *in* HUMAN HISTORY

What is Required of Japan To Become a World Leader

✺ 1 ✺

THE POWER OF WISDOM REQUIRED NOW

What I feel now, at the 25th Celebration Of Lord's Descent

This chapter is a transcript of the lecture I gave at the 2015 Celebration of Lord's Descent on July 7, seven o'clock in the evening. It was the first time in many years that the event fell on a date marked by three sevens in a row, which I felt had a very nice ring to it.*

Actually, in Heaven, the number seven symbolizes completion and is also the number for victory. Thus, it would bring me the greatest happiness if this "777" would be engraved in people's hearts not only as the date for the Celebration of Lord's Descent, but also as the number for victory in this world.

The Celebration of Lord's Descent started in 1991 and this lecture marked its 25th anniversary. I asked the staff not to mention or write about my age at the time of the celebration, as I feel that my spirit still remains about the age of 40 and I do not really agree with the idea of a "retirement age" in our society. I would not like my age to go up every year; rather I prefer it to stay the same.

In Heaven, you can freely set your age. So, you can be as young or as old as you like. In this sense, you are constrained in this world, because people can only go in one direction when aging. But I intend to do my utmost to go against this and accomplish as much work as I can.

---

* The author was born on July 7, 1956 at around 7 in the morning.

With the help of many, I want to bring the Laws
To all people of the world

I said that this was our 25th Celebration of Lord's Descent; actually it was also the 25th anniversary of our official approval as a religious organization. Although I have been doing my best all along, from the viewpoint of my mission, I feel I have accomplished very little. I am filled with sorrow about this.

I had only given about 2,300 lectures and I had only written 1,902 books [at the time of the lecture]. At this pace, the Truth cannot reach all people of the world. Besides Japanese, I have some ability to give lectures in English, but like most people, no matter how much I study, if I study English I forget other languages and if I study other languages I forget English. At this very slow pace, unfortunately it is not possible for all people of the world to hear my teachings directly from me while I am still alive.

In this respect, I need the support of many people and, even if it is in an indirect manner, I want to spread the Laws to the entire world. I would be happy if you could spread even a part of my teachings, the ones that you think are most important.

Internationally, Happy Science has been expanding to a great extent, but unfortunately we are short of staff and branch offices to accommodate the growth. Also, since each country has its own culture and educational background, we have some difficulty in conveying the Truth. Sometimes we find many people to be at a level where they simply do not have the capacity to absorb the teachings; they are struggling to survive or in the midst of conflict. They are struggling and are still at a level quite far from learning high-level teachings. This means that even though this lecture had been broadcast via satellite simultaneously around the world and people listened to it on the same day, there was a big difference in how much each listener understood my teachings.

The kind of wisdom you attain is important

I often give lectures focusing on Japan, so I hope the people of Japan understand that they have much more responsibility compared to people of other countries. That is the meaning of my birth in this country.

Japan now has the world's third highest GDP, but it is doubtful whether it has the capabilities to become a leader of the world and whether it is indeed fulfilling that role. Just as I do not yet have enough strength, this country still lacks strength as well.

I am not referring only to "power" when I say "strength," but also "wisdom." The world is in turmoil and confusion because it lacks clear wisdom. If you have clear wisdom, you can make decisions. And if you can make decisions, things will get done. In this respect, the kind of wisdom you attain is extremely important. This is the first point I would like to make.

✣ 2 ✣

A SPIRITUAL REVOLUTION THAT ENCOURAGES PEOPLE TO MAKE A GREAT SHIFT IN PERSPECTIVE

The two major streams of thought in the world

Happy Science started its activities centered on religious reformation and religious revolution. The main purpose of these activities was to launch a spiritual revolution. In simple terms, spiritual revolution means to encourage people to acknowledge themselves as spiritual beings first. It also means to encourage people to live each day while examining their way of life from such a perspective. This great shift in perspective will be the major turning point in how you live as human beings.

There are two major streams of thought in the world today. One constitutes people who believe that this material world is the only one that exists. The other constitutes people who have faith and believe in the existence of God, Buddha, angels, tathagatas, bodhisattvas and high spirits. Each country is situated somewhere between these major streams of belief. This is the present situation of the world.

So, where does this country, Japan, lie? In the 70 years after Japan lost the Greater East Asia War, or World War II, we have recovered economically, but not sufficiently in terms of mental attitude. Unfortunately, this is the current situation of Japan.

I was born 11 years after the war, in 1956. Recognizing the timeliness of my birth, I can clearly see that I was born with the aim of leading the recovery and prosperity of Japan and, through this recovery and prosperity, to extend a hand of salvation to the world.

The significance of the Greater East Asia War

I would like to say a few words regarding the views of history that people have held for 70 years since World War II. The current public opinion in Japan is based on a masochistic view of history where citizens believe that Japan did awful things during the war; the postwar period began with this feeling of remorse. People a generation older have this kind of thinking. They believe that this was how Japan was able to do well during these 70 years, so they feel the need to preserve this way of thinking.

Of course, self-reflection, itself, is not a bad thing. But in so doing, the Japanese have rather tormented themselves and often caused themselves suffering and misery. The Japanese tended to have a negative outlook, which prevented them from being proactive toward others and doing altruistic deeds. It is undeniable that they have long adhered to such "one-country pacifism," which actually worked in a positive manner to promote the well-being of a small country.

However, thinking about how the Japanese have progressed 150 years since the Meiji Restoration and how Japan has a long uninterrupted history of over 2,000 years, the masochistic view they have retained for the last 70 years is severely lacking. After all, there must be a mission appropriate for such a nation's capability.

It is very hard, at this point, to confirm facts that happened in the past. There would probably be many opinions and many details. However, as a religious leader, I have been holding firmly to one point: I have been saying that the Greater East Asia War was not solely the responsibility of the Japanese emperor, who was the head of state according to the old constitution, nor the Japanese politicians and soldiers that ignored the emperor. The Japanese Shinto gods had a clear aim to liberate the colonies of the world. Regarding this point, I have not wavered once. This is the only way to think about it. The fighting took place under this objective.

Certainly, more than three million Japanese died during World War II. Nevertheless, it is true to say that their fighting served as a great force to encourage the colonies in Asia and Africa to gain independence after the war. For Japan, this was probably not a perfect outcome, but for the world, it brought a better reality. This is one aspect of truth.

The term "peace" has different meanings Depending on the country

In this country Japan, public opinion is still wavering right and left. I have no intention of criticizing people who are at the extremes, nor do I intend to say that people who cannot understand divine will are inferior. Making decisions is a very difficult thing to do as long as we live as humans in this world, because everything has strengths and weaknesses, or positive and negative outcomes. It is up to each person to choose one conclusion from many options. This is a truly difficult thing to do. So I neither intend to deny everything nor approve everything.

Having said this, Japan must make a decision that will allow its future to continue. Japanese actions and way of living should also be an example for the people of other countries. These should serve to guide other countries. I believe this is the mission that Japan is assigned now.

Recently, the Abe administration, mainly led by the Liberal Democratic Party, has debated national security legislation and tried to reassess postwar Japan. There has been heated debate in the Diet, in public opinion and in the mass media. I believe it is a good thing that different opinions come up; we need to discuss matters thoroughly to reach a conclusion that will leave us with no regret.

Nevertheless, I must tell you one thing. The word "peace" has multiple meanings. While there are countries that take the meaning of peace in a similar way as Japan does, there are also countries which take peace to mean getting benefit or gaining power at the expense of other countries. The difference in these opinions needs to be reconciled at the international level.

But above that, rather than just concentrating on the discussion between humans, I believe there is a great significance in knowing what the gods in Heaven think. Take, for example, Indian Justice Pal [see Figure 3]. Although he was not Japanese, in his spiritual messages he said more than a Japanese would have said. His comments were very favorable to Japan, which made me feel truly grateful. He complimented the Japanese so much that it was almost embarrassing. The Japanese need to reflect on whether they truly deserve such assessments of their moral standards.

Figure 3.
A photo of Justice Pal of India, who alone asserted that all of the defendants were not guilty at the International Military Tribunal for the Far East (Honorary monument at Yasukuni Shrine).

In his spiritual messages, he commented that Japan had been a leading power in the Orient and ought to become a leader of the world. Refer to Ryuho Okawa, *The Truth about WWII: Justice Pal Speaks on the Tokyo Trials* (Tokyo: HS Press, 2015).

✒ 3 ✑

UNDERSTANDING THE CONFLICT IN VALUE SYSTEMS OF THE WORLD

Difficult situations the world superpower America will face from now on

What we can do now is to decide on how we should pave the way into the future and in which direction we should lead the world. For example, at the end of 1990s, there was a widely held opinion that the 21st century would be the century of America and that its superiority would be guaranteed for over a hundred years, so we would just need to follow the one and only superpower, America. However, in just over a decade, the world situation has shifted from a one-country superiority to one where multiple powers exist. This shift in the world is very complicated and is difficult to fully discern.

From America's standpoint too, it will be very challenging for it to remain a superpower. For example, President Obama referred to equality in his inauguration address and the U.S. finally legalized gay marriage by establishing same-sex marriage laws. The country rejoiced that homosexuals and heterosexuals would be treated equally and celebrated it as "a great victory," with the White House lighted up in rainbow colors.

This is no doubt a blessing for a certain percentage of people who are or have been discriminated against and I believe it is very important to give thoughts to this minority in the world, so that they do not have to suffer. But from another standpoint, I also believe it is true that, as Japanese Shinto gods say, a civilization will meet its end if same-sex marriage becomes the major trend in that era.

While it is important to protect the rights of the minority, if the number of homosexuals increases and they become the majority, civilization will decline. This is inevitable, because there would be no meaning for men and women to be born on earth and there would be no purpose in leaving descendants. This is one major issue America will face from now on.

What is more, America has the issue of being a gun society. In the U.S., people are being killed in various places because they can own guns freely; we cannot just follow suit. The same goes for drugs in U.S. society. I understand that America is a society that is overstressed from competition, but a society where drugs are so widespread that people can use them as easily as smoking cigarettes is an ailing society.

In addition, there is the issue of racism, which is connected to the previously mentioned views on war. Racism is still rooted very strongly and deeply inside America, so I feel that America has not finished reflecting on this yet. Americans will need to reflect on their centuries-old history of racial discrimination.

Therefore, we cannot accept everything America does just because it is a developed country. There are things we should and should not accept. During the era that Chinese civilization was more advanced than others, there were things that Japanese society did and did not accept from China. In the same way, there are ways of thinking that are widely held in a certain country, but should not spread to other countries.

German frustration regarding compensation
For the financial crisis of Greece

Furthermore, as we look over the entire world, we anticipate a very difficult time in terms of future international politics. For example, Greece nearly defaulted on its debt in July 2015 and talks have continued as to whether or not Greece should leave the European Union.

Greece is a country with only one twenty-fourth the economic power of Japan. The Greek economy is of a scale where Japan could go in and help right away, if it wants to. But there is an ongoing argument in the EU. Why is this? Actually, they are arguing over the difference in their ways of thinking.

According to one international economist, after people in Greece work until the age of 50, they can receive a pension that amounts to 75 percent of their salary at the time of retirement.* If this is the case, they could live the rest of their lives at ease, which is truly wonderful for the Greek people.

However, these pensions come from money borrowed from other countries in Europe. For this reason, it is natural that some countries in the EU cannot tolerate that. At the center of this frustration is Germany. In Germany, the pension paid at retirement age in the 60s is about half of their salary. This means that even if people work 10 years longer than those in Greece, they will get paid only 50 percent. So, why should Germany lend Greece so much money to let the Greek people live a comfortable life after retirement and why should Germany accept the fact that the money will not be repaid? These are the points they are arguing about.

---

* This was stated by Japanese economist Keitaro Hasegawa. In principle, the legal retirement age in Greece is 65, but 70% of all workers retire early between ages 51 and 61.

Their frustration is understandable. People who do not work much can receive more than 70 percent of their salary and can retire 10 years earlier, while people who work 10 years longer only receive half of their salary and have to bail out other countries as well. It is only natural that Germans will not stay quiet about this and, the EU, of which Germany occupies a central position, cannot easily assent, either. That is why the EU demands that Greece undertake fiscal austerity.

On the other hand, people in Greece are opposed to adopting such a measure because it will make their lives worse. Indeed, Greece is suffering from a very high unemployment rate. So, we can see a conflict of value systems here.

A split has been appearing in the EU due to Increased unemployment caused by fiscal austerity

In reality, unemployment rates in Europe have been very high. But unemployment further increases if stricter fiscal austerity is imposed, as has been done, by decreasing the amount of money in circulation and trying to achieve fiscal reconstruction.

This is why, unfortunately, German Chancellor Merkel's way of thinking, focusing on fiscal austerity, does not necessarily accord with the mainstream idea of the economists. She is a physicist from the former East Germany and thinks in the same way as former Japanese Prime Minister Naoto Kan during Japan's prior Democratic Party administration.

Although the prime minister of Greece is very extreme in his comments, honestly speaking, Chancellor Merkel does not seem to understand international economics, either. In fact, both sides may have their say, but both are problematic. Therefore, a split has been appearing in the EU.

China's actions could lead to the world Splitting in the future

There is a possibility that China and Russia will aid Greece, further breaking the EU apart. Here lies a trend where the world could again split in two. America will of course be supporting the EU.

There are similar situations elsewhere. For example, there is extreme tension in the Philippines and Vietnam in response to China artificially reclaiming a coral reef in the Spratly Islands to construct a military base [see Figure 4]. In addition, in Thailand, a military government has emerged and America has imposed severe economic sanctions against it. For this reason, Thailand is trying to buy three submarines from China. China has thus gotten a firm foothold in Thailand. So, if China were to get into a conflict with the Philippines or Vietnam, the countries of Southeast Asia would not act in unison.

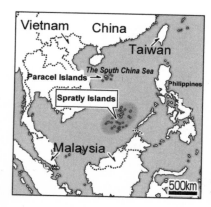

Figure 4.
Various countries surrounding the Spratly Islands, including Vietnam, China, Taiwan and the Philippines, claim that the islands are their own territorial ground. Since 1980s, China has coercively expanded effective control over these islands, inviting reproach from international society.

Neither constitutionalism nor the rule of law is almighty

What about Thailand's neighbor, Burma [Myanmar]? Burma is now ruled by a military government as well.* To prevent Ms. Aung San Suu Kyi from becoming president, the military government has added a provision to their new constitution with wording similar to, "Anyone who has married a foreigner cannot become president. Neither can anyone who has had a child with a foreigner become president. In addition, anyone who has not served in the military cannot become president." Japan is now arguing over its own interpretation of constitutionalism, but if people adhere to the constitutionality of Burma, Ms. Suu Kyi cannot become president.

It is possible to do such things with a constitution. It is possible to add articles to it to prevent a particular person from becoming president. This is a huge problem. After all, the problem lies in the people who make the laws, not the laws themselves.

China declares itself to be a country governed by law. For example, it has recently set up new security related laws, such as the National Defense Mobilization Law in 2010 and National Security Laws in 2015. In accordance with these laws, China would call on Hong Kong, Macau and Taiwan to fulfill their duties and responsibilities to safeguard national security as Chinese territories as well as exercise government authority on the Internet.

What is more, foreigners who build factories, open shops or start companies in China cannot go against Chinese authority. For example, if China engages in a war that the Japanese government opposes and if a Japanese company located in China also takes the same posi-

---

* This was at the time of this lecture. Later, in the general elections held on November 8, 2015, Aung San Suu Kyi's National League for Democracy (NLD) won a victory and gained a majority of seats, ensuring that it would take power.

tion, that company could be forfeited. This kind of domestic law exists in China. This is possible under the legal system determined by China.

Therefore, the law is not almighty. Constitutionalism and the rule of law are merely the powers which arise from the common intelligence of the people who create them.

✒ 4 ✑

THE SPIRIT OF A RELIGIOUS NATION IS REQUIRED TO BECOME A WORLD LEADER

"Democracy without God" and "Democracy with God"

I have discussed various issues. To sum up, I believe that the Japanese people, as a whole, must raise their level of recognition and their understanding on the international community.

Happy Science publishes many spiritual messages. This is not only to inform people that the age of spirituality has arrived, but also to teach them that a democracy can mean a "democracy without God" or a "democracy with God." Furthermore, we describe what kind of human rights must be guaranteed in a democracy with God, in order to further raise the level of fundamental human rights and get closer to God.

This is what a religious nation is. By raising the level of fundamental human rights, people can continue their soul training in this world in an effort to get closer to God. The determination to make this country of Japan such a place and to make it a model for other countries is the spirit of a religious nation.

Unlike Greece, the Japanese economy is In no danger of bankruptcy

There are also quite a number of economic problems in Japan, but the Japanese people have more than 1,700 trillion yen [approx. 14 trillion dollars] in personal assets. Although Japan is said to have a debt of over 1,000 trillion yen, its citizens hold more than 1,700 trillion yen in assets and they hold 95 percent of the national debt. This means that, unlike Greece, Japan is not in danger of going bankrupt.

The Japanese government says that citizens will leave a legacy of debt for their descendants, or talks about the indebtedness of the country and its citizens. But what the government says is partially incorrect. Actually, the government is the one in debt, whereas the citizens have credit against the government. In other words, it is not correct to say that the citizens have a debt of eight million yen per person; the actual situation in Japan is that each citizen is owed eight million yen by the government, with even more personal savings on top of that credit.

Furthermore, Japan is the world's largest creditor nation in terms of foreign trade and surpassed China once again as the holder of the most U.S. bonds in the world [as of February 2015]. This means that Japan, in this current situation, cannot stall economically or sharply decline.

What the Japanese government must do now is Job creation

Japan must do what it must while it still has the time to do so. What is it that Japan must do? It is not to cover one loan by taking out more loans. Japan should not do what Greece is doing. Japan is different from Greece, where the government uses the money borrowed from foreign countries to run its administration. Former Prime Minister Naoto Kan could not understand this and warned people that Japan would end up like Greece, but this would not actually happen to Japan.

What the Japanese government must do while its citizens buy government bonds with their savings is job creation. It must make diligent efforts to create new jobs. As for the citizens, they must work to build a society which produces jobs that allow people to work until at least 75, or even older, rather than retiring at 60. This is the direction the world needs to head toward for the future.

Starting with establishing a religious nation, I hope that every one of you will undergo the most fruitful soul training on this earth and complete your spiritual discipline successfully. I sincerely pray from the bottom of my heart that when you return to the Real World, you will become great beings who are close to God and can guide people in all areas of the world.

WORK TO REALIZE PEACE ACCOMPANIED BY JUSTICE

Atheism and materialism are wrong.
These ideas must not be used
As the principles of politics
And the principles of education.
While it is important to advocate peace in politics,
That act must not let evil forces get stronger.
We must never forget
To consider the perspective,
"What is justice?"
This perspective is necessary to reduce evil
And increase righteousness on this earth.
Justice has the effect
To restrain devils' forces from spreading on earth
And to educate them.
I must teach peace that is accompanied by justice.

Peace that gives in to evil,
Peace that is controlled by evil
And peace that reconciles with evil
—This is peace with dishonor.

It is natural for each ethnic group or country
To want to protect its people
And to hope for its own peace.
However, from the grander perspective
Or from the global level,
We must constantly explore and examine,
"What is justice?"
"What is righteousness?"
"What is Truth?"

For example,
It is not wrong for people in Hiroshima and Nagasaki,
Who suffered the atomic bombings,
To make a vow
That humanity shall never again commit such acts
And officially voice that these acts are wrong.
Rather, those people should make a vow
And let their voice be heard.
At the same time, however,
These efforts must not lead them
To nurture a weak mind
That allows the forces
Who are still making atomic bombs
And threatening other countries
To be left free and to get stronger.

Those who aspire to tell people
How tragic the war was
And how countless people were in misery
After the atomic bombings
Must, at the same time,
Give strict but fair criticisms to the forces
That are aiming to start a new war.
Those who are preparing themselves
To start one
Shall have no freedom to criticize in any way
The peace and history of other countries.

After all,
We must constantly think
About what accords with righteousness
On a global level
And from the perspective of the future.

From *The Essence of Buddha – On Politics*

Chapter 6

ESTABLISHING the JUSTICE of GOD

The Teachings of the Supreme God, Now Needed by the World

✤ 1 ✤

THE WORLD'S VALUE SYSTEMS
ARE NOW WAVERING

American-type global justice is now in question

The final chapter of this book is entitled, "Establishing the Justice of God." Although it is questionable whether anyone on earth is entitled to speak on such a theme, I will try to address this topic the best that I possibly can. I feel this subject needs to be addressed because the world's value systems are starting to waver.

In 1991, the Soviet Union collapsed, giving an impression that the battle between the liberalist countries and the socialist countries had ended. Around that time, most people were thinking that America would establish its supremacy as a superpower and lead the world, and that globalism, with America as its central force, would sweep across the world.

This view was prevalent in the 1990s and, on seeing that trend, I also slightly modified the forecast I previously made. In fact, earlier, I predicted that in the first half of the 21st century, America would be in danger of collapsing, but I decided to alter my prediction to say that America's political power would probably continue for more than a hundred years and throughout the 21st century in order to align with the world's trends.*

Nevertheless, I now have the impression that there has been a reversal of this trend and the world seems to be heading toward real-

---

* In the first edition of *The Golden Laws* (Tokyo: HS Press, 2015), published in Japanese in August 1987, there was a section predicting that around the year 2000, New York, the former center of the world, would be devastated to the point it nearly loses its function.

izing my first prediction. Until very recently, it was generally believed that global justice, or God's justice, would be defined according to American standards, and that there would be no mistake as long as we followed their judgment. However, this stance has become rather doubtful, and questions and various objections are now being raised against American standards from various quarters.

The standard for judgment must be the realization of The greatest happiness of the greatest number and The happiness of later generations

There are also extremely difficult issues arising in terms of the management and administration of the world as a whole. Quite a large number of variables have been emerging as unknown factors, not only in human society, but also in changes of the Earth's environment, including natural disasters. If we simply consider natural disasters to be divine punishment, then what seems to be divine punishment is occurring in many regions of the world. Even if we were to consider the issues in human society to be the only topic of discussion regarding justice, we can see that people's views on what is right and what is wrong are wavering, for example, in law and economy.

Various discussions have taken place, especially within Japan, which marked its 70th anniversary, in 2015, since the end of World War II. Many debates have arose from topics such as the ideal form of state, national justice, the difference between global justice and national justice and the correct way to perceive what Japan did more than 70 years ago from the view of world history.

When opinions on a certain issue are totally divided, there is always some truth on either side, which means that there is no opinion that is 100% true, nor is there one that is absolutely false. There is always some truth in both. One approach to decide what justice is at the present point in time is, for example, to think about how to bring the greatest happiness to the greatest number of people. Or, when deciding whether something is right or wrong, we should consider whether our decision will enable the humankind of the future to maintain the right ethical standards of living.

Two contradicting ideas in democracy

We are in an era where democracy is the central force at work, but I would like to point out that there are contradicting ideas in democracy as well. Democracy as taught in simple terms in elementary school holds that what is supported by the majority vote is right, and school-wide decisions such as class representatives or the theme for the school festival are selected accordingly. However, democracy also contains the idea that the rights and views of the minority must be protected, or people who have different ideas must also be treated with tolerance.

In fact, the latter concepts of democracy contradict the first approach of simply making a numerical comparison to decide which is correct. If what is right is always decided by what is supported by the greatest number, it could mean that all the actions of the country with the largest population are basically right. Yet, a universal Truth or an aim to achieve a high ideal could lie in an opinion of a minority or an individual. The Truth in such an opinion must be followed, even if the majority does not support it.

✒ 2 ✑

IS THE EVALUATION OF JAPAN IN TERMS OF WORLD WAR II JUST?

Asia's positive remarks on Japan are not reported fairly

In March 2015, I published a new book, *Palau Shoto Peleliu-to Shubitaicho Nakagawa Kunio Taisa No Reigen* [English title, *For the Love of the Country: Untold Story of the Battle of Peleliu: A Memoir of Japanese Colonel Kunio Nakagawa*](Tokyo: IRH Press, 2015). The following month in April, the emperor of Japan visited the Palau Islands to console the spirits of the 10,000 Japanese soldiers who died on Peleliu Island [see Figure 5]. It was probably out of his long-cherished wish that he decided to go on such a trip at the age of 81; he must have felt his duty as the emperor to visit there.

The Republic of Palau gained independence in 1994. The president at the time, Kuniwo Nakamura, was of Japanese descent; he had a Japanese father. He strongly believed that in the United Nations, a

Figure 5.
On April 9, 2015, the emperor and empress of Japan visited the Palau Islands out of their long-cherished wish, to offer flowers at the monument of the soldiers who died during the Pacific War. Later, Empress Michiko commented that the trip left an unforgettable impression on her because they could finally offer prayer for the souls of both the Japanese and American war dead.

vote by Palau should be just as significant as that by America and China. He also said, "Why do Japanese apologize so much when we feel nothing but gratitude toward them? Why do you belittle yourselves like that and say what you did was wrong, when Japan actually fought to defend us?"

Despite that, not one Japanese politician attended or raised the Japanese flag at the first anniversary of Palau's independence because the prime minister of Japan at that time was the leader of the Socialist Party, Tomiichi Murayama. Apparently, the president of Palau was very sad about this and even commented that the people of Palau were grateful for Japan to have fought to assure their prosperity [see Figure 6].

China currently has around 1.3 to 1.4 billion people, so by majority rule, what they say may seem right. Nevertheless, the tiny nation of Palau has one vote too, just like China.

The people of India and Sri Lanka also have positive feelings toward Japan, just as people in Palau do. They say that if Japan had not

Figure 6.
In March 2015, the Happiness Realization Party Leader, Ryoko Shaku (left), visited the war ground on Peleliu Island at the Republic of Palau, where she paid her tribute to the souls of the war dead. Shaku also met the former president of Palau, Kuniwo Nakamura (right). He commented that, as a president, he would eternally be grateful of Japan.

fought, they would not have gained their independence. In Thailand too, there was the postwar Prime Minister Kukrit Pramoj, who had wrote an article giving thanks to Mother Japan for all nations of Asia gaining independence, back when he was a journalist.

Thus, in Asia, there are different opinions on Japan, but they have not been reported fairly. This shows how difficult it is to assess the past correctly, even when it is over.

The reason why I proactively voice My opinions on global issues

While it is difficult to assess the past correctly, it is more difficult to evaluate what is happening in the present appropriately, and even more so when it comes to the future.

A few days ago, I was reading a book on international politics. At the beginning of the book, the head editor had written that the study of international politics does not give a clear explanation of current issues, because it does not reach any conclusion. This may be true, but it is also a form of avoiding taking responsibility.

When an international conflict or war breaks out, if the experts who have done research on the matter cannot express an opinion on what is right and what is wrong, how can ordinary people be expected to do so? I think they are hiding behind the curtain of academia. Someone who has studied the history of international politics should be prepared, as an expert, to shoulder a certain amount of risk and voice what he or she thinks about the current situation and its prospect.

Usually, people who speak out and express various opinions on these matters are called "critics" who do not belong to an organization. They voice various opinions, but their level of influence differs from person to person; sometimes their opinions are put aside as insignificant. To put it another way, those who are only responsible for their own family are able to speak their opinions freely, but whether their opinions will or will not be accepted is another story; it depends on the discretion of the mass media, government agencies or politicians.

I speak out proactively on global issues too, but unlike critics and scholars, there is a certain degree of responsibility that comes with what I say. This is because there are many people who follow me believing what I say is true and many of them make political decisions or decide what action to take based on my comments. In that sense, I have to be extremely cautious. But at the same time, I tell myself that being cautious must not mean running away or neglecting my responsibilities. It would have been meaningless to have established Happy Science if I were to simply try to protect our group by hiding behind a system that does not hold me responsible.

It has been about 30 years since the establishment of Happy Science. Although we are stable in some ways, we sometimes do things that involve risks. This is why we may well experience some clashes in value systems. Although people make decisions based on their own views or religious sense of values, I must express my opinions on those decisions as well. The time has come for me to say what I believe must be said, regardless of whether people will accept it or not. Whether or not my opinions will be accepted depends on the efforts of our believers and on the number of non-believers who nonetheless agree with me. But at the very least, my opinions now have certain influence on the course of this country, Japan.

Since nothing in this world is perfect, I, too, may have had some mistakes in my ideas or understandings, or lacked some consideration toward others. Even so, I intend to keep on stating what I believe should be done to bring common good to the greatest number of people.

Even the victor nations cannot change
The culture and religions of the defeated nations

Recently, and especially since we started giving teachings about Japanese Shinto through our spiritual messages, I have found that there is a certain trend going on. Happy Science is certainly not a right-wing religion that simplistically upholds State Shinto. I am sure you understand that. If we were a right-wing organization that only upholds State Shinto, we would scarcely approve the value of Christianity and of Islam, or acknowledge certain righteousness in Judaism or show understanding for Buddhism and other ways of thinking.

Happy Science has fully recognized that there have been good features and ideas in other religions as well and that they fulfilled their purpose in a particular era or geographical region. This attitude remains unchanged. In the same line, we are now trying to restore the value systems stated by Japanese Shinto religion. This is because, from a global perspective, I find many elements in the current decisions and evaluations made against Japan to be unreasonable.

It is true that in war, the victor gains overwhelming power and can rule over the loser. However, there are limits to what is acceptable and what is not.

Things such as culture, traditions and religion are unique to national identity and are unchangeable; they are on a different dimension from the question of which country is stronger in a war. For example, Britain ruled India for about 150 years, but it could not change the religion of India. Although Christianity spread slightly, the vast majority of people in India kept their traditional religion of Hinduism, and the British could not change that.

Similarly, European Christian missionaries began visiting Japan in the 1500s. Around the same time, European firearms were introduced into Japan, changing the form of warfare and spreading the influence of Western civilization. A huge revolutionary movement occurred with the Meiji Restoration in the mid-1800s as well, but even today Christians still remain less than 1 percent of the population in Japan.

Although Japan saw Western civilization as a good thing and adapted it during the Meiji Era [1868–1912], Christianity did not spread. What is more, Christianity has not spread throughout Japan, even though it lost in World War II and was occupied. Although there were some ideas in Christianity that were right, it did not spread because Japan already had its own ideas. Happy Science is now clarifying these ideas, as people lacked clarity on exactly what they were.

The spiritual background of outbreaks of war, And the historical rise and fall of nations

In terms of religion, the era of monotheistic religions has continued for two or three thousand years now and there is a tendency to consider monotheism to be pure and non-monotheistic religions to be muddled and defiled. Of course, there is nothing wrong with monotheistic religions that worship a universal God who loves all humankind, but there are also those that worship a specific god who only protects one particular ethnic group. Forcing other ethnic groups to believe in their own god would mean that one particular group could completely dominate others. That would be unreasonable.

On this issue, Happy Science teaches that there are different levels of gods, and there are also ethnic gods. In fact, different countries have their own ethnic god, whose role is to bring prosperity and wealth to the people of that specific country, and to guide them in the right way. When some particular countries make progress and gain national strength, or in other words, when four or five powerful countries emerge, cultural friction arises and competition occurs between ethnic gods, each striving to prove whose teachings would be able to better guide humankind to happiness as well as bringing prosperity to a country. When this competition exceeds a certain point, a war sometimes breaks out.

Looking back in human history, there were many major wars. Those wars were all tragic. There is no such thing as a non-tragic war. They all ended in tragedy, no matter which side people were on. But at the same time, world history shows us that through major wars, great nations sometimes rise and sometimes perish; a dominant country would go into decline and another great power would emerge, thereby resulting in a change of age.

We see many such occurrences on a small scale in everyday society. Various companies prosper greatly at times, yet at other times, they go under and are replaced by other companies. A similar principle is at work in the rise and fall of countries. While, in the case of war, human lives are at stake, which is a serious matter, in the case of competition between companies, people will suffer financial problems by losing jobs. Of course, they could perish if they lose their jobs and can no longer feed themselves, so it is true that financial problems could also lead to death.

Looking solely at the world trend over the past two or three thousand years, some countries began competing against one another whenever they grew larger and stronger. Then, wars would break out.

This kind of trend probably will not disappear so easily. There is also a tendency that the more fervently countries engage in military reduction, the more likely it is for a war to break out as a repercussion. In many cases, military reductions are imposed on weak countries by powerful ones as limiters to prevent opposition. This leads to a buildup of resentment in weak countries, which often resorts to expansionist policies. In that sense, military reductions are not always effective and are extremely difficult matters to deal with.

৵ 3 ৲

HOW TO VIEW CLASHES BETWEEN DIFFERENT RELIGIOUS CIVILIZATIONS

The significance of the increase In the number of Muslims

I have made various comments about international politics. In this section, I would like to consider things from the perspectives of today's international politics and religion. From a religious perspective, issues involving Islam cannot be overlooked. The situation is still fluid and will continue to fluctuate, so it is difficult to think about it definitively, but I would like to start with the conclusion.

There are supposedly around 1.6 billion Muslims throughout the world. Slightly older references note there were 1 billion or 800 million, so there is no doubt their numbers are increasing. Islam is very widespread among the world's poor, especially in poverty-stricken regions. So, in some ways it may be spreading as a substitute for communism and socialism in the past. Thus, as Islam is spreading among the needy, we could say that it is spreading within communities that are struggling to overcome the status quo, but have little hope of improving their condition.

On the other hand, Christianity is said to have 2 to 2.2 billion believers, so it is true to say that Islam is drawing close. I am not so sure about what Christians say outwardly but historically, they have considered Islam to be the teachings of the devil. That seems to be their true feeling. It may appear that way if you look at things from a worldly perspective and focus too much on the differences between one religion and the other. However, we can be assured that the teachings of the devil would not spread to more than one billion people.

Judaism only has a little over 10 million believers so, numerically speaking, Judaism would have to be destroyed in a battle between Judaism and Islam. Islam is now being criticized because some extremists are conducting many dreadful acts of terrorism, but the number is still increasing. Accordingly, there must definitely be aspects of Islam that cannot be understood with Christian values.

The reasons for Western men and women Joining the Islamic State as volunteer soldiers

The worst problem regarding Islam would most probably be the Islamic State. More than 60 countries have encircled the Islamic State and are trying to destroy it. Once the battle begins, there will be no end to it unless it comes to an absolute end. So, all we can do is to see how far it will go. I am not sure if the Islamic State has an organized structure that can negotiate a ceasefire. But there may not even be ceasefire if the situation turns into a mere guerrilla warfare.

According to what I read in a recent issue of *Newsweek*, apparently at least 3,500 people from Western countries have entered the territory of the Islamic State to give it support and 2,500 of them have become its soldiers. *Newsweek* also observed that 20 percent of the 3,500 were female. Since this is a magazine published in the Christian world, I do not think the actual figures could be any lower. In fact, there is a possibility they could even be higher.

In short, the Islamic State must have something that attracts people from all over the world to join their volunteer army, even though the mass media constantly reports it as a terrorist organization. There can be no doubt that these recruits felt a sense of outrage in the way Christian countries have violated Islamic countries such as Iraq, Iran and Afghanistan. That is something that must not be overlooked.

So, if 3,500 people have crossed national borders to go and help the Islamic State, we should consider them to have at least a thousand times more supporters than that. This means there are bound to be more than 3.5 million people who support the Islamic State. What does this mean? This is actually a matter of how much you are allowed to intervene against countries on the other side of the globe, or against people who have a different culture or who believe in a different religion.

Two heroes described in the movie, American Sniper

In the U.S., the movie *American Sniper*, released in December 2014, was a big hit; it even won the Academy Award for Best Sound Editing. The movie is about a real sniper who went to the Iraq War four times and shot more than 160 people. In the U.S., he is considered a hero. Apparently, he was originally a hunter and, as a sniper, was capable of hitting targets from a distance of more than 1,000 yards.

On the enemy side, there was also a sniper who had come from Syria to join the organization in Iraq that later became the Islamic State. He had won a gold medal in shooting at the Olympics and could also snipe from a distance of more than 1,000 yards. Apparently it is very difficult to shoot someone from more than 1,000 yards away, and it became a battle between these two men. Ultimately, the American sniper shoots and kills the Olympic gold medalist on the enemy side from a distance of more than a mile.

While he was regarded as a hero, and went to the battlefront in Iraq four times, he is said to have been a loving father at home. One day, back in America, he accompanied a fellow American to a gun range, only to be shot by him. This is a true story that happened in 2013. The U.S. held a state funeral for him, as a hero, followed by a long funeral procession. So, he was not killed in battle, but in his own country.

This is truly a difficult issue. In a war, someone who killed more than 160 of the enemy is indeed a hero. However, viewed from the enemy side or from the perspective of Iraq, those fighting against the American army in Iraq were defending their country. Although they might have been guerrillas, they were actually defending their country and its people and protecting their families. So, from the Iraqi point of view, they were the heroes.

It is very difficult to judge these two kinds of heroes. Can someone who comes from the other side of the globe and kills your countrymen be called a hero? He is certainly not a hero to the opposing side. In addition, the more strongly one side resists, the more aggressively the other side attacks. This is what usually happens. So, in many cases, it comes down to a power struggle. When things get so embroiled, value judgments start to waver.

The reasons extremists in Muslim countries Are driven to acts of terrorism

It is often said that there are no righteous wars. Nevertheless, I believe that, unless the attacker has a just cause that is totally understood and supported by the global community, the ones being attacked— the ones defending their own territory, people and families—are not necessarily evil.

This can be said of anything. For example, the biggest fear for animals is to be eaten by their predators. This is the same as being killed. In the natural world of animals, being killed and eaten is the biggest fear, though this experience is sometimes necessary for their soul training.

It is of course a different story if you attack a group that displays overwhelming savagery. But if that is not the case, the act of unilaterally condemning the other side for their differences in culture, ways of thinking and religion, is too extreme.

The problems with regard to the Islamic State will probably not come to an end yet, but at some point there will have to be a ceasefire. And I believe that a line must be drawn by providing those who do not agree with current regimes, especially Sunni Muslims, with some form of autonomy or right of residency.

I do not approve of the attitude, "Kill all who oppose." Both the Sunnis and the Shiites are proper religious sects that believe in Allah and follow the teachings handed down through Muhammad, so you cannot say they are completely wrong. Nevertheless, there are indeed aspects where the extremists make things worse. I feel Muslim extremists are doing a tremendous disservice to Islam as a whole by their actions which could mislead the world to think Islam is a religion that engages in terrorism.

I am well aware that Muslim extremists believe such acts are the only option available since they are considerably inferior in terms of their war potential. They cannot attack with fighter planes or aircraft carriers, so I can understand the reason why they can only use guerrilla tactics. However, when there are so many cases of suicide attacks by pregnant women wrapped in dynamite, or by children dispatched carrying explosives, or entire families charging in with car bombs, it cannot be helped if Islam is thought to be such a religion. But Muhammad's original teachings do not contain this extreme element.

❧ 4 ❧

IN ORDER FOR JAPAN TO CONTRIBUTE TO WORLD PEACE

The reasons why the Japanese "Special Attack" Units Depicted in the movie, The Eternal Zero, *Are not considered terrorists*

There is a prevailing opinion that says the Islamic extremist terrorists are copying Japan's Special Attack Units in World War II. There is a possibility it may have provided some sort of inspiration to them. However, the truth is that, as depicted in the movie *The Eternal Zero* [released in Japan in 2013] and the book it was based on, Japan's Kamikaze Unit did not commit acts of terrorism.

The Japanese actor Haruma Miura, who won Best Actor and Best Supporting Actor in the Japanese Academy Awards for this movie, played the role of a contemporary young man. In the movie, his friends asked him, "A Zero fighter crashing into an aircraft carrier is surely the same as a terrorist suicide bombing, isn't it? What is the difference?" And he said, "An aircraft carrier is a weapon of mass destruction, carrying many fighter planes and bombers. Crashing a plane loaded with explosives into it is not an act of terrorism, but an act of war; it is a battle between two weapons. It is different from terrorism, which targets and deliberately involves civilians." But his friends were unable to accept his argument. I remember this scene in the film.

Indeed, during World War II, in many ways the Japanese Army regarded the war basically as a confrontation between military forces. So, it is not accurate to say what they did were acts of terrorism.

I want people to understand the heart of Yamato, Which did not forsake Okinawa

Some people tend to perceive the Kamikaze Unit as total insanity, and after the war, the Japanese Imperial Army was criticized for having carried out such a reckless strategy. It is a fact, however, that the planes of the Kamikaze Unit sank or dealt damage to at least 300 American warships, mainly in the Okinawa area. So, although movies often depict that they were shot down in the sky and died in vain, this description is not correct. It was a great achievement to deal damage to over 300 battleships.

In fact, 50 percent of the Kamikaze fighters were shot down before they reached their target, but half of the remaining 50 percent that managed to survive through the bullets, or 25 percent of the total, hit their target and either sank or damaged more than 300 battleships. Among those who were sent on this kamikaze mission, many of them were notably from the Japanese mainland. I want the people of Okinawa to be aware of that fact.

When the land battle for Okinawa had begun, the Battleship Yamato cast off from Yamaguchi Prefecture for Okinawa alone, with no escort ships to guard it, as is shown in the movie, *Yamato* [released in Japan in 2005]. The battleship was sent based on a reckless strategy: destroy a fleet of enemy transport ships, beach itself and serve as a gun battery from which to shoot enemy ships. So, the battleship was not fueled enough to make a return trip, right from the beginning. But it was eventually attacked by enemy fighter planes before it reached its destination and sunk about 125 miles from Makurazaki in Kyushu.

The Battleship Yamato carried a crew of around 3,000, roughly the same number of people who died in the World Trade Center terrorist attack. The crew went down before reaching Okinawa, about 125 miles from Kyushu. They went to battle knowing that they would lose and sink.

Many in Okinawa say, "Yamatonchu [meaning "the people of mainland Japan" in Okinawan dialect] do not understand how Okinawans feel," but I would like for them to understand this heart of Yamato.* The Battleship Yamato was sent to sacrifice itself to show the people of Okinawa that they had not been abandoned. I really would like people to understand this.

Hegemonism that lacks a noble cause is wrong

With regard to World War II, some people in China believe that their land was ravaged for 10 or 20 years by the Japanese and think of Ja-

---

* *Yamato* in Battleship Yamato is the old name for Japan or Japanese people. It also means "great harmony."

pan as an evil empire. They may well have the right to think like that. However, that does not mean to say that today's People's Republic of China can do the same as they believe Japan did in the past.

It is meaningful to do research on the past. In regard to the so-called Nanking massacre and military comfort women, some stories tell that 300,000 people were killed in Nanking and that 200,000 were forced to work in military brothels. However, my judgment after spiritual research is that these stories are false [see Figure 7].

Having said this, even if we suppose those stories were true, that does not give China any good reason to continue increasing its military budget by more than 10 percent every year for 20 years. China is no doubt on its way to dominate Asia and the region as far as Hawaii. This is obvious. They may want to say, "Japan has no right to say anything because it did the same thing in the past. Japan must be silent; Japan has no right to say anything about us." But this thinking is mistaken. Hegemony without a cause is wrong.

Figure 7.

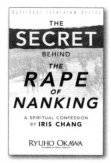

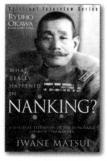

Ryuho Okawa, *The Secret Behind* The Rape of Nanking: *A Spiritual Confession by Iris Chang* (Tokyo: HS Press, 2014).

Ryuho Okawa, *What Really Happened in Nanking?: A Spiritual Testimony of the Honorable Japanese Commander Iwane Matsui* (Tokyo: HS Press, 2015).

Right now, Mr. Xi Jinping has imprisoned, detained or executed more than tens of thousands in the Communist Party ranks.* He has started to purge even colleagues who disagree with his opinions and, as we have seen in Hong Kong, has suppressed people seeking liberalization.

With regard to the Uighur region, too, Chinese authorities have announced that around 100 people have died, but there have been reports coming in from Uighur that, in actuality, thousands of people have been massacred. Thus, a system must be created to reflect the voices of the occupied territories, including Inner Mongolia, Uighur and Tibet.

Japan must gain power to protect itself And contribute to world peace

It is clear that China is aiming to invade countries like Nepal, too. But since Happy Science missionary work has been making progress there, the Maoist faction has become a minority and has adopted a defensive stance. Myanmar is similarly trying to avoid allying themselves with China. Sri Lanka had accepted Chinese investment to build a naval port, but suspended that project before it was completed. Sri Lanka changed its policy to align with America and Japan. I believe that, although small, my overseas lecture tours have played some role in this [see Figure 8].

My lectures also had the same effect in Australia as well. When I went to Australia to give my first lecture, the prime minister at the time, who had an approval rate of 90 percent, was proficient in Chinese and was leaning toward China. However, the next prime minis-

---

* At the National People's Congress of 2015, it was announced that about 55,000 government officials were investigated for corruption.

ter shifted closer toward Japan, out of fear that China would buy up Australia's natural resources. Australia has now adopted the stance of defending these resources [also see Figure 8].

This signifies that Japan has been Asia's model in the 70 years since the end of World War II. I believe it is right for Japan to have the power to defend itself. This power will enable Japan to prepare military deployment when required by the international society and will help Japan have a say at the global level. I believe it is important for Japan to contribute to world peace in this way.

People sometimes make mistakes. People sometimes lose wars. However, I believe people can acquire wisdom from losses. Countries that have never experienced this type of loss may not understand this.

Figure 8.
The author gave a lecture entitled, "Life and Death," in Nepal on March 4, 2011 (top left), and "The Power of New Enlightenment" in Sri Lanka on November 6, 2011 (top right). On March 29, 2009, he gave a lecture in Australia entitled, "You Can be the Person You Want to Become," and on October 14, 2012, "Aspirations for the Future World" (left).

❧ 5 ❧

OVERCOMING RELIGIOUS AND ETHNIC CONFLICTS

Monotheistic religions tend to speak ill of other religions

So, what should be done to overcome conflicts between religions? In the world, there is a rather widespread mindset, based on monotheism, which regards other religions as heretical. However, in many cases, this judgment comes from ignorance. People are simply thinking as they were taught in their religion.

It would seem that even church leaders are often limited to this level of awareness. In the course of their missionary work they enthusiastically preach that their beliefs are the only ones that can save people, and they gradually narrow their scope to say that there is no salvation other than through Jesus.

Nevertheless, I can well understand why religions tend to move in that direction. After all, people will not join their church unless they say that it is the only route to salvation. Happy Science does not say that people cannot enter Heaven unless it is through our organization, but I can understand as a historical principle that as time passes, people would want to say things like that. It is true that the more passionate people become, the more likely they tend to be like that.

Muslims have a similar passion. I can understand how they feel that they must fight to protect the Land of Allah against those who are trying to destroy Islam. They also feel that Muhammad was outnumbered by enemies, but overcame them and built a nation under Allah's Will. This is probably why they are trying to emulate him, though there are some differences between Muhammad's state of mind and theirs.

Buddhism and Japanese Shinto recognize various gods; Their idea is close to worshiping the Supreme God

In Buddhism, which is not considered monotheistic, many gods are present. The Buddhist way of thinking is that there are gods, in plural, but Buddha is above them in hierarchy. Given that Buddhism teaches that Buddha is above the gods, it is not monotheism but is rather close to the idea that there is the Supreme God.

Japanese Shinto has higher-ranking gods. In some cases, Ame-no-Minakanushi-no-Kami* is said to be the highest god, yet in other cases, Amaterasu-O-Mikami† is worshiped as the most exalted. But there are many other gods beside the supreme one and they assemble to discuss various issues. In other words, Japanese Shinto has held "national assemblies" since ancient times.

Shinto has an extremely democratic religious outlook. Of course the gods do not have assembly seats like in the Diet, but meet somewhere to discuss things on an equal footing; this kind of democratic religious outlook is, I believe, extremely rare. So, the gods of Japanese Shinto closely resemble human beings.

Judaism seen from the perspective of righteousness

How about Judaism? The Jewish nation originally came into being when Moses led the Exodus from Egypt. It is said that the Jews had

---

* The central god in Japanese Shinto. His name means "the central god of the universe."
† The supreme goddess in Japanese Shinto. She is said to be the direct ancestor of the emperor of Japan.

been enslaved in Egypt for around 400 years before they fled the country. While it is fairly amazing that today's Korean Peninsula had been under Japanese rule for around 35 years, 400 years is really a very long time. If we trace the Japanese history back 400 years or so, it would take us back past the Meiji Era to the early Edo Era. In other words, the period that the Jews spent in slavery is the equivalent of the time that has passed since Ieyasu Tokugawa established the Edo Shogunate in around 1600.

So, given that their god guided the Jews in such circumstance to flee from Egypt and had then built their own nation, we can presume that there must have been many biases in their ways of thinking. This being so, it is only natural that the Jews would speak ill of those around them. I can understand their god's intention in praising the Jews by telling them that they were better than everyone else, in an effort to give people who had been slaves the confidence to build their own country. Nevertheless, it is questionable whether these teachings are truly right.

Incidentally, in January 2015, *Exodus: Gods and Kings* was released in Japan. This is an American movie about the Exodus. While the Exodus had been depicted in the past in movies such as *The Ten Commandments*, now that computer graphics have advanced so much, scenes such as Moses parting the Red Sea and the drowning of the army of Ramses II are a spectacle to behold.

According to my book, the persecution of Moses occurred not during the reign of Ramses II, but during the reign of his son, Merneptah.* We believe that Moses and Merneptah were both brought up by Ramses II. On the contrary, Hollywood fixates on Ramses II and always makes it him who persecuted Moses. He was the most power-

---

* Refer to Ryuho Okawa, *The Golden Laws: History through the Eyes of the Eternal Buddha* (Tokyo: HS Press, 2015).

ful ruler in Egypt, so he makes a great antagonist. It differs slightly from historical truth, but making the strongest ruler the antagonist boosts Moses' appeal.

The time has come to revise
The criteria of justice on a global scale

Only in recent years has it become possible to think about things on a global scale. Until then, each group in each era made decisions based on its central ideas. So, in the past, when transport and communications had not developed, it was nearly impossible for people to think about things on a global scale. Even in Hitler's day, there was still a certain amount of distance between European countries. Now, the time has finally come when we can think about things on a global scale. Therefore, the criteria for justice will change from ethnically focused ones to more universal ones; whether something is right will be judged from an international perspective.

There are drawbacks to an approach that makes decisions based solely on numbers, too. The decision will differ depending on the style taken, for example, whether the population alone is taken into consideration or whether each and every country is considered to have one vote regardless of size. So, a purely numerical approach should not be adopted. After all, we must fully explore the theme, "What is right?"

Postwar justice is based on the belief that justice means preserving the systems of the victorious nations at the time World War II ended. Following that rationale, it has continuously been believed that it is wrong to change any system created by the World War II victors. However, even countries blessed with victory from the war have changed over 70 years. If some of those countries have faded or deteriorated and have come to nurture ways of thinking that would bring unhappiness to other countries, some kind of international system must work to check and restrain those countries.

It is fine to seek the help of the United Nations, for example, which already exists, but the problem is that Japan is not a permanent member of the Security Council at this time. Japan must become a permanent member. This is obvious. It is strange that China is the only Asian country to have a permanent seat on the Security Council. Japan can serve to unify the opinions of other Asian countries.

Related to this, in World War II, America rationalized its killing of Japanese people by calling them "yellow monkeys" and "Japs" and considered the conflict as a battle against devils. I would like America to reflect upon the fact that its wartime propaganda was overdone, though not to the extent that would destroy the relationship between the two countries, of course.

South Korea's slander of Japan Contains remnants of its ethnic consciousness

Since we are on the topic of Japan's relationships with other countries, I would also like to say a few words about South Korea. Japan needs to make efforts as well when it comes to Japan-South Korea relations, but a while ago the Japanese people were very accepting of South Korea, as a result of the rise in popularity of Korean pop culture. On the contrary, there seems to be a great amount of brainwashing going on in South Korea, since their politicians tend to try to gain popularity by speaking ill of Japan in order to raise their approval ratings.

As for North Korea, things have reached the level where there is no point talking with them. It is considered to possess as many as 100 nuclear warheads within five years, so something must be done about this soon.

South Korea indicted the former bureau chief of the Japanese *Sankei Shimbun* newspaper and prohibited him from leaving the country. There is a problem with those actions.* It might have been a problem if the *Sankei Shimbun* had outdone its competitors and scooped an article defamatory of South Korean leadership and knowingly risking its Seoul bureau being banned, but in fact, it merely wrote an article that followed a topic that had already been reported in South Korea. Despite that, its bureau chief was prevented from leaving the country for "libeling the president."

The article reported that when South Korea was in crisis after a luxury liner capsized and many people died, there was a seven-hour period when the president's whereabouts were unknown, and it posed the question of her location during that time. Whether it was a lover or a sweetheart was a mystery, but it was reported in South Korea that she may have been with someone. The *Sankei Shimbun* bureau chief picked up on those reports, and the authorities found fault with his article, indicted him and refused to let him leave the country. Japan could do nothing about it.

Furthermore, in South Korea, a novel became a bestseller since that summer. In the novel, An Jung-geun, the "hero" portrayed as shooting Japan's first Prime Minister Hirobumi Ito†, is resurrected in the current era for some reason and tries to kill Prime Minister Abe.

---

* The South Korean authorities prevented the former chief of the *Sankei Shimbun*'s Seoul Bureau from exiting the country and placed him under house arrest, saying that the article on the *Sankei Shimbun* website in August 2014 defamed President Park Geun-hye. Prosecutors asked for an 18-month prison term but on December 17, 2015, the Seoul Central District Court issued a verdict of not guilty. Finally, prosecutors decided not to appeal the court decision, thereby confirming that the former Seoul bureau chief is not guilty.

† Hirobumi Ito [1841–1909] was the first prime minister of Japan. He was assassinated in Harbin by An Jung-geun, a Korean nationalist and independence activist, after serving as the first Japanese resident-general of Korea.

The Japanese are a very unusual group of people who do not get angry about such things. Maybe it does not bother them that much to begin with because a politician's life is like a firefly light that can go out at any moment. While Japan did not complain about the glorification of a novel in which An Jung-geun is resurrected and attempts to assassinate Prime Minister Abe, in South Korea, a Japanese journalist was arrested for writing about something that had already been reported there. South Koreans may still bear a grudge toward former Japan, but the truth of the matter is that they are unable to go beyond their ethnic consciousness.

Earlier in this chapter, I mentioned the Kamikaze Special Attack Units. Apparently, some of their members included Koreans who had graduated from the military academy in Japan and were proud to take part in the attacks. So, both sides need to demonstrate more maturity and make some allowances in their discussions.

↙ 6 ↘

REALIZING HAPPINESS FOR ALL HUMANKIND BY ESTABLISHING THE JUSTICE OF GOD

God's justice is revealed in my books, The Laws of the Sun, The Golden Laws *And* The Laws of Eternity

Then, what are the criteria of justice that God upholds? The answers can be found in the flow of human history. God does not expect history to be something static and monotonous. People can sometimes become corrupt if they wield power for a long time. Organizations created by people can collapse after exceeding their effective periods, such as one, two or three centuries. Some say that a revolution occurs when an organization gets out of step with the times. Thus, God considers innovation a matter of course.

If people of the world want to know what God's justice is, I would advise them to read my books, *The Laws of the Sun* (New York: IRH Press, 2013), *The Golden Laws* (Tokyo: HS Press, 2015) and *The Laws of Eternity** and try to understand the philosophy in them. Reading all three books would not be so difficult; it certainly would not take a lifetime to read them. Reading speed may vary from person to person, but I think you can read them if you have a week or ten days.

By reading them, you can understand that there are different grades in gods: they range from the universal God that thinks about global justice, to gods that think about individual regions, countries or ethnic groups. You will also understand from the books that angels, prophets and messiah-like souls sometimes come down to earth and create a religion. In other words, there are differences between religions and each of those religions was founded to bring salvation to the people of its day and region.

Despite this, various wars and conflicts arise because certain beliefs are not suited to a different era, or to a different region's way of thinking. That is why I want to get rid of wars, conflicts and misunderstandings that arise from mutual ignorance. I am sure that once people of the world understand the philosophy taught in *The Laws of the Sun*, *The Golden Laws* and *The Laws of Eternity*, answers to many questions will become clear.

---

* Currently sold as *The Nine Dimensions: Unveiling the Laws of Eternity* (New York: IRH Press, 2012).

*In World War II, the separation of church
And state worked negatively*

Christian countries fought among themselves in World War II. America versus Germany, Germany versus France, Germany versus Britain; they are all Christian countries. As they killed one another, they probably said, "Lord, forgive me. Amen." They all fought in the name of God, so this was an unfortunate situation for all involved.

Jesus said something that could be taken as the basis for the separation of church and state: "Render therefore to Caesar the things that are Caesar's, and to God the things that are God's." However, I feel that this separation of church and state had a negative effect.

I wonder what would have happened if there had been no separation of church and state, and they had to strictly follow Christ's words in politics. Given that diplomacy is an extension of politics and war is an extension of diplomacy, if they had kept the spirit of Christianity alive in wartime as well, they would not have been able to engage in such senseless slaughter. However, in reality politics had become separated from religion, and that may have worked negatively.

*God's management works beyond
The borders of religions in each country*

The roots of Islam and Japanese Shinto are surprisingly similar, and they share some commonalities. They both believe that someone close to God should rule a country. Both have a profusion of war gods. In that sense, they are very similar. I intend to gradually clarify the parts that are common to Japanese Shinto, Islam and Judaism.

I have also confirmed the spiritual truth that the souls of Christian saints are being reincarnated as leaders of various other religions in Japan. People cannot transcend their nationality so easily, but some souls transcend nationality and move surprisingly freely around the world.

Let me explain this in terms of a company. There are different departments, some of which are weak and some are strong. In a company, efforts are made to ensure that everything goes smoothly overall by transferring personnel, who to send to which department. The same kind of effort is observed in the religious world. This is a reflection of "God's management."

What I want to say is this: the biggest desire of God is for many people—or if possible, everyone without exception—to live in happiness.

The Supreme God desires to realize
The happiness of all people

Many scholars who specialize in international politics often use a parable from Christianity to explain the principle of politics. They say that if one sheep out of a flock of 100 goes astray, the principle of politics would be to lead the remaining 99 sheep to safety, whereas the principle of religion would be to search the countryside for the one that has gone astray.

However, what I teach at Happy Science is different. I do not tell people to save the one lost sheep even if it means ignoring the 99. I say that you must also protect the 99 while caring for the lone sheep. Maybe I am asking for too much, but I tell people to do both. In other words, while we aim for the greatest happiness of the greatest number of people, we have to care for those who have slipped through the safety net, too. Please note, I am not saying that we have to organize everything around the latter.

The recent "Piketty Hypothesis" from France condemns widening income inequality, and it proposes to level everything in accord with the poor. However, that is nothing but Marxism; it would only make the whole world poor. In a world of poverty, people would no longer be able to help one another, so we should not aim for poverty. It is impossible to distribute wealth unless there is affluence. So, there must not be a mistake in your fundamental way of thinking. That is to say, it is wrong to construct an entire theory for the sake of one lost sheep.

Religion began to decline at the same time that Marxism appeared, and that is because Marxism includes part of a fundamental principle of religion. In fact, Marxism politically amplified the idea, "Right is on the side of the weak."

In reality, there can be no government, or management, without the support of the majority. This is true according to the principle of governance. Therefore, it is necessary to pay attention to both the wealthy and the poor in a well-balanced way.

God wishes for the prosperity of each country, as well as a global prosperity that brings harmony to all affiliated countries in the same age. When conflicts, contradictions or raging wars arise due to different ways of thinking, adjustment will naturally work to bring about reconciliation and produce peace. Someone may rise to oppose war or an angel of light may appear as a brave politician or soldier to crush those who commit evil. In this way, a principle will work in various ways to stop such conflicts.

While the principle of utilitarianism aims to achieve the greatest happiness of the greatest number of people, God actually hopes to realize the happiness of not just the majority of people, but of everyone. God constantly sends various leaders to earth with the aim of realizing what has yet to be accomplished. I would like you to be aware that this kind of "God's management" is carried out at the global level.

This is what Happy Science is teaching. I believe that as the teachings of Happy Science spread around the world, people will be able to deepen their mutual understanding and make better decisions by carefully considering what needs to be done. At the same time, if there are countries that only think of their own benefit and violate other countries, we must do our best to forcibly resist and stop them.

Happy Science is aiming to overcome the conflicts between atheistic, materialistic countries and countries that have faith, and to resolve hatred caused by the differences in religions around the world. We want to be a religion that continues to voice the message, "Transcend hatred and embrace love."

KNOW WHAT IS TRULY RIGHT

It may seem as if the Japanese mass media
Have the freedom to report whatever they wish,
But there are different levels within them.
A clear line is now forming
Between media that receive the blessings of God
And those that do not.
Of course, this is so,
Because Happy Science has been making clear
What is good and what is evil.
Regulating speech to deny God, Buddha,
Spirits or the Spirit World
Is the same as succumbing
To the current political systems
Of China and North Korea.
We are working hard in pursuit of religious Truth.

At the same time,
We are also striving
To gain political freedom and political rights,
And to create Utopia on this earth, every day.
In doing so, we must never forget the following:
"Think about what is right
From the perspective of God.
Based on that, decide the political policies
And the direction this country should take."
The answer is written in the countless books
I have published.

I wish to say to people all over the world.
Happy Science states opinions on justice
As well as what defies it.

Some parts of what we say
May conflict with a country's political system,
Economic system
Or attitude toward faith.
However, please be an adult.
Please be an adult
And know well what is truly right.
The future of Earth will open up
In the direction that my finger points.
We must continue to fight
Until the day that global justice is established.

From *What is Global Justice?*

AFTERWORD

With this book, I have gone beyond the boundary of academics. Put another way, I could say that I took on the challenge to make God's revelations a subject of academic studies.

I depicted an image of how justice should be in this world, as seen from the standpoint of God or Buddha. In doing so, I have surpassed the academic knowledge of prominent scholars in Japan and in the world, as well as the awareness of prime ministers and presidents. Some of you will feel the presence of God on a global level.

The Laws of Justice will have tremendous influence on various academic fields we have today. Furthermore, it will have a ripple effect on the future world, an effect beyond imagination.

I hope for the people, who assume religion is nothing more than a simple superstition or brainwashing, to reflect on their own ignorance and lack of education. This book is the DNA that will create our future society.

Ryuho Okawa
Founder and CEO of Happy Science Group
December 2015

*This book is a compilation of the lectures,
with additions, as listed below.*

- Chapter 1 -
God is Never Silent
Lecture given on December 16, 2014
at Happy Science General Headquarters, Tokyo, Japan

- Chapter 2 -
Conflict Between Religion and Materialism
Lecture given on November 10, 2013
at Tokyo Shoshinkan, Tokyo, Japan

- Chapter 3 -
Progress that Starts from Righteousness
Lecture given on January 24, 2015
at Yokohama Shoshinkan, Kanagawa, Japan

- Chapter 4 -
The Principle of Justice
Lecture given on May 24, 2015
at Head Temple Shoshinkan, Tochigi, Japan

- Chapter 5 -
The Great Turning Point in Human History
Lecture given on July 7, 2015
at Saitama Super Arena, Saitama, Japan

- Chapter 6 -
Establishing the Justice of God
Section 1-4: Lecture given on March 8, 2015
at Tokyo Shoshinkan, Tokyo, Japan
Section 5-6: Excerpts from its Q&A Session

* *Contemplative Quotes* are taken from other books and a Q&A session by the author.

About the Author

Ryuho Okawa is a renowned spiritual thinker, leader, and author in Japan with a simple goal: to help people find true happiness and create a better world. To date, Okawa's books have sold over 100 million copies worldwide and been translated into 28 languages. His books cover essential teachings such as how our thoughts influence reality, the nature of love, and the path to enlightenment.

In 1986, Okawa founded Happy Science as a spiritual movement dedicated to bringing greater happiness to humankind by uniting religions and cultures to live in harmony.

Happy Science has grown rapidly from its beginnings in Japan to a worldwide organization. The spiritual workshops Happy Science offers are open to people of all faiths and walks of life and are rooted in the same simple principles of happiness that inspired Okawa's own spiritual awakening. Okawa is compassionately committed to the spiritual growth of others; in addition to writing and publishing books, he continues to give talks around the world.

In addition to promoting spiritual growth, Okawa has also dedicated himself to improving society and creating a better world. As affiliates of the Happy Science Group, he has founded various institutions including boarding schools, a higher education institution, a preschool education institution, as well as a publishing company, a political party, a talent agency, and a talent school.

For more information about the activities and services of each institution, visit happy-science.org/activities/group.

What is a Spiritual Message?

We are all spiritual beings living on this earth. The following is the mechanism behind Master Ryuho Okawa's spiritual messages.

1 You are a spirit

People are born into this world to gain wisdom through various experiences and return to the other world when their lives end. We are all spirits and repeat this cycle in order to refine our souls.

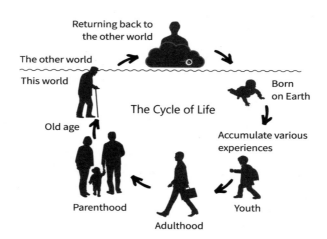

Returning back to the other world

The other world

This world

Born on Earth

Old age

The Cycle of Life

Accumulate various experiences

Parenthood

Adulthood

Youth

2 You have a guardian spirit

Guardian spirits are those who protect the people who are living on this earth. Each of us has a guardian spirit that watches over us and guides us from the other world. They were us in our past life, and are identical in how we think.

The other world

Guardian Spirit

This world

Watches over us/ sends us inspiration

You

3 How spiritual messages work

Since guardian spirits think at the same subconscious level as the person living on earth, Master Okawa can summon the spirit and find out what the person on earth is actually thinking. If the person has already returned to the other world, the spirit can give messages to the people living on earth through Master Okawa.

1 The guardian spirit / spirit in the other world...

2 Goes inside Master Okawa in this world

3 Master Okawa speaks the words of the guardian spirit / spirit

The spiritual messages of more than 600 spirits have been recorded by Master Okawa since 2009, and the majority of these have been published. Spiritual messages from the guardian spirits of living politicians such as U.S. President Obama, Japanese Prime Minister Shinzo Abe and Chinese President Xi Jinping, as well as spiritual messages sent from the Spirit World by Jesus Christ, Muhammad, Thomas Edison, Mother Teresa, Steve Jobs and Nelson Mandela are just a tiny pack of spiritual messages that were published so far.

Domestically, in Japan, these spiritual messages are being read by a wide range of politicians and mass media, and the high-level contents of these books are delivering an impact even more on politics, news and public opinion. In recent years, there have been spiritual messages recorded in English, and English translations are being done on the spiritual messages given in Japanese. These have been published overseas, one after another, and have started to shake the world.

For more about spiritual messages and a complete list of books in the Spiritual Interview Series, visit spiritualinterview.com

About Happy Science

Happy Science is a global movement that empowers individuals to find purpose and spiritual happiness and to share that happiness with their families, societies, and the world. With more than twelve million members around the world, Happy Science aims to increase awareness of spiritual truths and expand our capacity for love, compassion, and joy so that together we can create the kind of world we all wish to live in.

Activities at Happy Science are based on the Principles of Happiness (Love, Wisdom, Self-Reflection, and Progress). These principles embrace worldwide philosophies and beliefs, transcending boundaries of culture and religions.

Love teaches us to give ourselves freely without expecting anything in return; it encompasses giving, nurturing, and forgiveness.

Wisdom leads us to the insights of spiritual truths, and opens us to the true meaning of life and the will of God (the universe, the highest power, Buddha).

Self-Reflection brings a mindful, nonjudgmental lens to our thoughts and actions to help us find our truest selves— the essence of our souls—and deepen our connection to the highest power. It helps us attain a clean and peaceful mind and leads us to the right life path.

Progress emphasizes the positive, dynamic aspects of our spiritual growth—actions we can take to manifest and spread happiness around the world. It's a path that not only expands our soul growth, but also furthers the collective potential of the world we live in.

Programs and Events

The doors of Happy Science are open to all. We offer a variety of programs and events, including self-exploration and self-growth programs, spiritual seminars, meditation and contemplation sessions, study groups, and book events.

Our programs are designed to:

- Deepen your understanding of your purpose and meaning in life
- Improve your relationships and increase your capacity to love unconditionally
- Attain a peace of mind, decrease anxiety and stress, and feel positive
- Gain deeper insights and broader perspective on the world
- Learn how to overcome life's challenges
  … and much more.

For more information, visit happyscience-na.org or happy-science.org.

International Seminars

Each year, friends from all over the world join our international seminars, held at our faith centers in Japan. Different programs are offered each year and cover a wide variety of topics, including improving relationships, practicing the Eightfold Path to enlightenment, and loving yourself, to name just a few.

Happy Science Monthly

Our monthly publication covers the latest featured lectures, members' life-changing experiences and other news from members around the world, book reviews, and many other topics. Downloadable PDF files are available at happyscience-na.org. Copies and back issues in Portuguese, Chinese, and other languages are available upon request. For more information, contact us via e-mail at tokyo@happy-science.org.

Contact Information

Happy Science is a worldwide organization with faith centers around the globe. For a comprehensive list of centers, visit the worldwide directory at happy-science.org or happyscience-na.org. The following are some of the many Happy Science locations:

United States and Canada

New York
79 Franklin Street
New York, NY 10013
Phone: 212-343-7972
Fax: 212-343-7973
Email: ny@happy-science.org
website: newyork.happyscience-na.org

Los Angeles
1590 E. Del Mar Blvd.
Pasadena, CA 91106
Phone: 626-395-7775
Fax: 626-395-7776
Email: la@happy-science.org
website: losangeles.happyscience-na.org

Orange County
10231 Slater Ave #204
Fountain Valley, CA 92708
Phone: 714-745-1140
Email: oc@happy-science.org

San Diego
Email: sandiego@happy-science.org

San Francisco
525 Clinton Street
Redwood City, CA 94062
Phone/Fax: 650-363-2777
Email: sf@happy-science.org
website: sanfrancisco.happyscience-na.org

Florida
12208 N 56th St.,
Temple Terrace, FL 33617
Phone:813-914-7771
Fax: 813-914-7710
Email: florida@happy-science.org
website: florida.happyscience-na.org

New Jersey
725 River Rd. #102B
Edgewater, NJ 07020
Phone: 201-313-0127
Fax: 201-313-0120
Email: nj@happy-science.org
website: newjersey.happyscience-na.org

Atlanta
1874 Piedmont Ave. NE
Suite 360-C
Atlanta, GA 30324
Phone: 404-892-7770
Email: atlanta@happy-science.org
website: atlanta.happyscience-na.org

Hawaii
1221 Kapiolani Blvd., Suite 920
Honolulu, HI 96814
Phone: 808-591-9772
Fax: 808-591-9776
Email: hi@happy-science.org
website: hawaii.happyscience-na.org

Kauai
4504 Kukui Street
Dragon Building Suite 21
Kapaa, HI 96746
Phone: 808-822-7007
Fax: 808-822-6007
Email: kauai-hi@happy-science.org
website: happyscience-kauai.org

Toronto
323 College Street,
Toronto, ON M5T 1S2
Canada
Phone/Fax: 1-416-901-3747
Email: toronto@happy-science.org
website: happyscience-na.org

Vancouver
#212-2609 East 49th Avenue
Vancouver, V5S 1J9
Canada
Phone: 1-604-437-7735
Fax: 1-604-437-7764
Email: vancouver@happy-science.org
website: happyscience-na.org

International

Tokyo
1-6-7 Togoshi
Shinagawa, Tokyo, 142-0041
Japan
Phone: 81-3-6384-5770
Fax: 81-3-6384-5776
Email: tokyo@happy-science.org
website: happy-science.org

London
3 Margaret Street,
London, W1W 8RE
United Kingdom
Phone: 44-20-7323-9255
Fax: 44-20-7323-9344
Email: eu@happy-science.org
website: happyscience-uk.org

Sydney
516 Pacific Hwy
Lane Cove North,
2066 NSW
Australia
Phone: 61-2-9411-2877
Fax: 61-2-9411-2822
Email: aus@happy-science.org
website: happyscience.org.au

Brazil Headquarters
Rua. Domingos de Morais 1154,
Vila Mariana, Sao Paulo,
CEP 04009-002
Brazil
Phone: 55-11-5088-3800
Fax: 55-11-5088-3806
Email: sp@happy-science.org
website: cienciadafelicidade.com.br

Jundiai
Rua Congo, 447,
Jd.Bonfiglioli,Jundiai- CEP 13207 - 340
Phone: 55-11-4587-5952
Email: jundiai@happy-sciece.org

Seoul
74, Sadang-ro 27-gil,
Dongjak-gu, Seoul, Korea
Phone: 82-2-3478-8777
Fax: 82-2-3478-9777
Email: korea@happy-science.org
website: happyscience-korea.org

Taipei
No. 89, Lane 155, Dunhua N. Road
Songshan District
Taipei City 105
Taiwan
Phone: 886-2-2719-9377
Fax: 886-2-2719-5570
Email: taiwan@happy-science.org
website: happyscience-tw.org

Malaysia
No 22A, Block2, Jalil Link
Jalan Jalil Jaya 2, Bukit Jalil
57000, Kuala Lumpur
Malaysia
Phone: 60-3-8998-7877
Fax: 60-3-8998-7977
Email: Malaysia@happy-science.org
Website: happyscience.org.my

Kathmandu
Kathmandu Metropolitan City,
Ward No. 15, Ring Road, Kimdol,
Sitapaila,Kathmandu
Nepal
Phone: 97-714-272931
Email: nepal@happy-science.org
　　　nepaltrainingcenter@happy-
　　　science.org

Uganda
Plot 877 Rubaga Road Kampala
P.O. Box 34130
Kampala, Uganda
Phone: 256-79-3238-002
Email: uganda@happy-science.org

About IRH Press USA Inc.

IRH Press USA Inc. was founded in 2013 as an affiliated firm of IRH Press Co., Ltd. Based in New York, the press publishes books in various categories including spirituality, religion, and self-improvement and publishes books by Ryuho Okawa, the author of 100 million books sold worldwide. For more information, visit OkawaBooks.com.

Follow us on:
Facebook: MasterOkawaBooks
Twitter: OkawaBooks
Goodreads: RyuhoOkawa
Instagram: OkawaBooks
Pinterest: OkawaBooks

Other Books by Ryuho Okawa

IRH Press

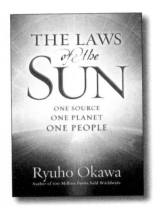

THE LAWS OF THE SUN
One Source, One Planet, One People

ISBN: 978-1-937673-04-8
$24.95 (Hardcover)

IMAGINE IF YOU COULD ASK GOD why He created this world and what spiritual laws He used to shape us—and everything around us. In *The Laws of the Sun*, Okawa outlines these laws of the universe and provides a road map for living one's life with greater purpose and meaning. This powerful book shows the way to realize true happiness—a happiness that continues from this world through the other.

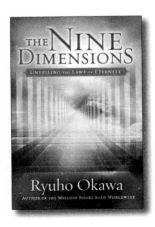

THE NINE DIMENSIONS
Unveiling the Laws of Eternity

ISBN: 978-0-9826985-6-3
$15.95 (Paperback)

THIS BOOK IS YOUR GATE TO HEAVEN. In this book, Master Okawa shows that God designed this world and the vast, wondrous world of our afterlife as a school with many levels through which our souls learn and grow. This book is a window into the mind of our loving God, who encourages us to grow into greater angels.

THE HEART OF WORK
10 Keys to Living Your Calling

THINK BIG!
Be Positive and Be Brave to Achieve Your Dreams

INVITATION TO HAPPINESS
7 Inspirations from Your Inner Angel

MESSAGES FROM HEAVEN
What Jesus, Buddha, Muhammad, and Moses Would Say Today

CHANGE YOUR LIFE, CHANGE THE WORLD
A Spiritual Guide to Living Now

THE MOMENT OF TRUTH
Become a Living Angel Today

SECRETS OF THE EVERLASTING TRUTHS
A New Paradigm for Living on Earth

For a complete list of books, visit okawabooks.com.

HS Press

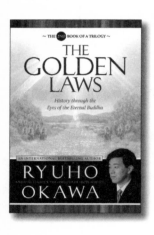

THE GOLDEN LAWS
History through the Eyes of the Eternal Buddha

ISBN: 978-1-941779-81-1
$14.95 (Paperback)

The Golden Laws reveals how Buddha's Plan has been unfolding on earth, and outlines five thousand years of the secret history of humankind. Once we understand the true course of history, we cannot help but become aware of the significance of our spiritual mission in the present age.

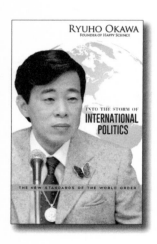

INTO THE STORM OF INTERNATIONAL POLITICS
The New Standards of the World Order

ISBN: 978-1-941779-27-9
$14.95 (Paperback)

The world is now seeking a new idea or a new philosophy that will show the countries the direction they should head in. In this book, Okawa presents new standards of the world order while giving his own analysis on world affairs concerning the U.S., China, Islamic State and others.

THE LAWS OF WISDOM
Shine Your Diamond Within

THE LAWS OF PERSEVERANCE
Reversing Your Common Sense

THE LAWS OF GREAT ENLIGHTENMENT
Always Walk with Buddha

RYUHO OKAWA: A POLITICAL REVOLUTIONARY
The Originator of Abenomics and
Father of the Happiness Realization Party

SPIRITUAL MESSAGES FROM
THE GUARDIAN SPIRIT OF RYUHO OKAWA
The Divine Voice of Shakyamuni Buddha

THE TRUTH ABOUT WWII
Justice Pal Speaks on the Tokyo Trials

FOR THE LOVE OF THE COUNTRY
Untold Story of the Battle of Peleliu:
a Memoir of Japanese Colonel Kunio Nakagawa

A SPIRITUAL INTERVIEW
WITH THE LEADER OF ISIL, AL-BAGHDADI
Including a Spiritual Investigation into the Truth
of the Japanese Hostage Taking

THE SECRET BEHIND *THE RAPE OF NANKING*
A Spiritual Confession by Iris Chang

THE TRUTH OF THE PACIFIC WAR
Soulful Messages from Hideki Tojo, Japan's Wartime Leader

WHAT REALLY HAPPENED IN NANKING?
A Spiritual Testimony of the Honorable Japanese Commander Iwane Matsui

Available at Amazon.com